MAYBE ONE DAY

Jeannette Gerstl Olson

To Lisa, Jeff, Jolie, and Elana,
With my very best wishes,
Jeannette Olson
Nov. 7, 2013

Maybe One Day

First edition, 2013
Copyright © 2013 by Jeannette Gerstl Olson

Library of Congress Cataloging-in-Publication Data on file
ISBN 978-1-4675-8873-7

With Contributions by:

Stacey Olson Sachs
Graphic Design Consultant and Photo Editor

Hilary Olson Mechler
Technical Analyst

Charles Michael Al-Dairy
Book Layout

Cover Design by Stacey Olson Sachs

Printed by Edwards Brothers Malloy
2500 South State Street
Ann Arbor, Michigan 48104

About the Cover

Inspired by the many photos my grandmother so diligently protected, this book cover brings together memories from before, during, and after the war. The front cover shows my grandparents and mother in happier times. The images behind them, faded but connected, represent carefree moments with friends and family before the Holocaust. Toward the bottom of the page, the photos separate, revealing a map of Nazi-occupied France. One glimmer of hope shines through this horrific chaos, with my mom in the loving custody of her surrogate parents and protectors, Emile and Lily Lasfargues.

The back cover represents new beginnings: Mom, Grandma and Papa's reunion with Lily, as well as the subsequent reunion of Grandma and Papa with Mrs. Picco, surrounded by photos of events that may never have been without the sacrifice of these courageous people. Black and white photos are followed by full, bright and vibrant color photos of children, grandchildren, aunts, uncles, and cousins…the many descendants and close friends of William and Pauline Gerstl. This is their legacy, as "maybe one day" became "today."

Stacey Olson Sachs
Daughter of Jeannette Olson

. . .

German and French signs in a restaurant window, Paris, Rue de Choiseul, September 1, 1940

**In this establishment
Jews are <u>not welcome</u>**

Exclusively Aryan Enterprise

*Jews
are <u>not admitted</u>
here*

IN ANY CASE

— Wislawa Szymborska —

Translated from the Polish by Grazyna Drabik and Sharon Olds

It could have happened.
It had to happen.
It happened earlier. Later.
Closer. Farther away.
It happened, but not to you.

You survived because you were first.
You survived because you were last.
Because alone. Because the others.
Because on the left. Because on the right.
Because it was raining. Because it was sunny.
Because a shadow fell.

Luckily there was a forest.
Luckily there were no trees.
Luckily a rail, a hook, a beam, a brake,
A frame, a turn, an inch, a second.
Luckily a straw was floating on the water.

Thanks to, thus, in spite of, and yet.
What would have happened if a hand, a leg,
One step, a hair away?

So you are here? Straight from that moment suspended?
The net's mesh was tight, but you? Through the mesh?
I can't stop wondering at it, can't be silent enough.
Listen,
How quickly your heart is beating in me.

WHAT MAKES THE HOLOCAUST STAND OUT FROM ALL OTHER GENOCIDES AND MASS MURDERS IN HISTORY

Besides the scale of the slaughter, there are two really unique and interrelated characteristics that differentiate the Holocaust from all other genocides and mass murders in history:

(1)   The level of industrialized, mechanized, and automated death. Never before, and, never since, has a mass murder campaign been carried out with such precision. Complete systems of automated death were designed and used to maximum efficiency, with constant "improvements" of the manufacturing processes. Unlike all other genocides, the level of planning and execution mirrored that of an industrial assembly line process to manufacture a product; in this case, the product was automation for death.

(2)   The level of which the Holocaust was institutionalized and bureaucratized by a nation's government to carry out their campaign. The reason we know so much about the Holocaust's victims was, that unlike all other mass-murder campaigns, the Nazis kept meticulous records of everything, just like any other government bureaucracy. A whole government ministry was set up to handle the killing, and did so like any other ministry — it competed for funding, talent, and resources, had goals and projections and produced statistical reports, and had all the hallmarks of "ordinary" government ministries. No other genocide has ever had this level of organization and official recognition within an established government the way that the perpetrators of the Holocaust had.

This industrialization of death is what truly differentiates the Holocaust from all other genocides. Other genocides have specifically targeted and killed minority groups in massive numbers, and with terrible means. However, no one else has ever directed the entire means of a modern industrial society and its technology for the purpose of genocide.

Source: *www.Answers.com*

TABLE OF CONTENTS

Dedication 9

Special Thanks 10

Family Members and Key Individuals 11

Author's Introduction 15

A Summary of Our Family's Survival During World War II 18

WWII Timeline Related to *Maybe One Day* 27

Chapter I: Vienna 1938 31

Chapter II: Kristallnacht (Night of Broken Glass) 39

Historical Information: The Aryanization Process 42

Chapter III: The Briefcase 49

Map: The Geographic Journey 56

Chapter IV: Crossing No Man's Land 57

Chapter V: Antwerp 1939 61

Chapter VI: Camp at St. Cyprien, Pyrénées-Orientales, France 65

Historical Information Camp St. Cyprien, France 71

Chapter VII: Camp Frémont, Vallon-en-Sully, France 75

Camp Gurs, Basses-Pyrénées 87

Letters from Camp at Gurs 88

Letters Willy and Paula 91

Chapter VIII: Escape 113

Chapter IX: Avenue Villermont, Nice 119

Chapter X: Hotel Pompeia 129

Italian Occupation of France 1942 137

Chapter XI: Vence Part I 139

Chapter XII: Nice Revisited 141

Chapter XIII: Vence Part II 145

Chapter XIV: The Attic 149

Chapter XV: 1944 The Liberation 153

Chapter XVI: Recollections of a Little Girl 159

Chapter XVII: Vence Post War 161

Chapter XVIII: A New Beginning 167

Letters: Lily to Jeannette 173

Correspondence: Max Bender and Hermine Bender 179

Historical Information: Riga, Latvia 210

Epilogue 216

Statistics: How many Jews Were Deported to the Death Camps from France? 220

My parents in 1988, Oak Park, Michigan

My husband Jerry and me in 2007

DEDICATION

My mother saved every document and letter regarding my father's and her experiences during the Holocaust. She had no particular plan; she just couldn't part with the memories, even though they were painful. I wrote *Maybe One Day* to preserve her memories, and to give purpose to the now-yellowed and frayed paper trail that she left behind. I dedicate this book to her and to my father, William and Pauline Gerstl, and I want to express my gratitude for their love, fortitude, wisdom and courage that saved our lives. I further dedicate this book to the following beloved people in my life:

My children, Sheldon Mark Olson, Stacey Ellen Olson Sachs, Susan Joan Olson Bitnias, and Hilary Helayne Olson Mechler, and their spouses, Adam Lloyd Sachs, Jeffrey Bitnias, and Charles "Chip" Mechler;

My grandchildren, Maxwell Spencer Olson, Joseph Isaac Olson, Justin William Sachs, Jonah Lyndon Sachs, Aidan Lee Sachs, Louis Paul Light, and Jordin Cherna Lily Mechler;

My cousin Cécile Gerstl Gruenwald, with whom I share many memories, and my cousin, Ruthe Gutstein Bardos, who, during my growing years, was my confidante, my role model, and my mentor. I further dedicate this book to their respective families.

I wrote this book in memory of my grandmother, Hermine Bender, and my uncle, Max Bender, who perished in 1941 at the hands of the Nazis;

Late aunts and uncles who went through the WWII journey with us: Ernst and Grete Gerstl, Hilda and Henry Gerstl, Joseph Schié Gerstl; Rosa and Ludwig Holzer, and my paternal grandmother, Maria Johanna Gerstl;

My late uncle and aunt, David and Paula Gutstein, who were instrumental in helping us get established in our new country, the United States;

My parents' rescuers, Delphin and Antoinette Picco, and Eugene and Marguerite Francone. Without their courage, I might never have known my wonderful biological family. I further wish to honor their children, Andrée Blumet and Jean-Pierre Francone and their families;

Lily and Emile Lasfargues who saved my life. Before reuniting with my mother and father, they had become my surrogate parents whom I loved and trusted;

Our rescuers in Nice: The Labress, Ginerolli, Borelli and Lolata families;

Family members I never had the privilege to know, who lost their lives because of the Holocaust.

Finally, I dedicate this book to family members of the future. My hope is that you will remain true to the lessons of the Holocaust. We remember those who perished, our ancestors who wished for nothing more than a peaceful life. Generation to generation, with knowledge and remembrance of this heinous event comes an obligation to stand up to intolerance and protect those who can't protect themselves. That is the lesson. God willing a peaceful life will be your legacy.

SPECIAL THANKS

To you, Jerry, my wonderful husband who saw me through this endeavor, encouraged me, listened to me, offered sound advice and help whenever I needed it, and stood by me all the way. Had it not been for my mother who refused to move back to Vienna, I would probably have married someone else and never have known the Joy of Jerry Olson.

To my daughter Hilary, your input was immeasurable. So often, you patiently explained computer techniques to me from Boston with little Jordin at your feet competing for your attention, while I, oh so slowly, fumbled my way through your instructions at my desk in Michigan. We traveled to France together in 2008 with our husbands, where we stepped back in time visiting Frémont in Vallon-en-Sully; the Piccos' home in Vence; the city of my birth, Nice; Antibes where I was hidden; and best of all, we spent time with Andrée [Francone] Blumet and her family in Lyon. Sharing this experience with you and our companions was one of the highlights of my life. Your touch and your heart are in this book.

To my daughter Stacey, God has gifted you with magic. Your talent escalated non-stop from the moment you drew your baby shoes in a high school art class, to your medical illustrations that have been published in medical books, and to your many beautiful murals in prominent Washington DC localities. You helped me in so many ways in making this endeavor come to fruition. Our incredible pilgrimage to France with you and Adam, summer of 2013, was an unforgetable emotional experience. Best of all, you have wrapped your grandparents' story in a wonderful book cover that you lovingly created.

To my son Sheldon and my daughter Susie, for your encouragement and standing by me whenever I needed you. Shel, you are blessed with an extraordinary sense of order which results in an incredible ability to multi-task and come up successful with the many challenges that face you on a daily basis. Through the years, with your outstanding computer skills and expertise, you provided me with the necessary training, tools and advice that enabled me to take on this project and complete it. I couldn't have done it without you. Susie, your laughter and sense of humor kept me upbeat during the hours, days, weeks, months, and years that I was involved in writing about the unfortunate past that almost destroyed our family. I knew that I could count on you for encouragement and help, and that meant a lot to me.

"Maybe One Day" is our legacy to the flowers that are growing on our family tree, and to the offshoots that will someday emerge. How blessed I am to have such a wonderful family — I love you all.

• • •

FAMILY MEMBERS AND KEY INDIVIDUALS

[Alphabetically listed by first names]

Antoinette and Delphin Picco — Rescuers who hid my parents in Vence, France, in 1943-1944. Parents of Marguerite Francone

Cécile Gerstl Gruenwald — Uncle Ernst and Aunt Grete Gerstl's daughter

Eugene and Marguerite Francone — Rescuers in Vence, France, 1943-1944

Ernest Gerstl [Ernie, Ernst] — My father's brother

Grete Sali Gerstl — Uncle Ernie's wife

Henry and Hilda Gerstl — My father's brother and his wife

Hermine Baeck Bender — My maternal grandmother

Jeannette Gerstl Olson — I am the daughter of William and Pauline Gerstl

Joseph Gerstl [Schié] — My father's brother

Lily and Emile Lasfargues — My rescuers who hid me in Antibes, France, in 1943/1944

Lisl Shapira — Aunt Grete Gerstl's sister

Maria Johanna Gerstl [Mémé] — My paternal grandmother

Max Bender — My mother's brother

Paula Gerstl Gutstein and David Gutstein — My father's sister and her husband

Pauline Bender Gerstl [Ma, Paula] — My mother

Rosa Gerstl Holzer and Ludwig Holzer — My father's sister and her husband

Ruthe Gutstein Bardos — Tante Paula and Uncle David Gutstein's daughter

Ruthi Gerstl — A five-year-old cousin who lived with my parents for a few months in Vienna in 1938

Sigmund Bender — My maternal grandfather

Therese Bender Scheer [Resi] — My mother's sister

Wilhelmina Bender Herbeck [Mimi] — My mother's sister

William Gerstl [Wilhelm, Willy, Willi, Pop, Papa] — My father

My gratitude to the Gineroli, Labress, Borelli, Lolata, and Mueller families who hid us in Nice, France, in 1942. Only Mr. Gineroli and Mrs. Mueller are mentioned in this book.

Not mentioned in this memoir are Laura Gerstl Scharfberg and Leo Scharfberg, my father's sister and her husband, who escaped Vienna to what was then Palestine and thankfully did not experience the horrors of Nazism.

Linguistic Conventions

I use my initials "JO" in this interview. Aunts are referred to as "Tante." Lily Lasfargues is sometimes referred to as "Tantine." "Mme" refers to Madame or "Mrs." " M." refers to Monsieur or "Mr."

MY GRANDPARENTS

My maternal grandmother, Hermine Bäck Bender, circa 1922.

My maternal grandfather, Sigmund Bender, circa 1922.

My paternal grandmother, the only grandparent I ever knew, Maria Johanna Gerstl [Mémé], circa 1925. Her husband, Samuel, was her first cousin.

Samuel Gerstl, my paternal grandfather, circa 1900.

MY MOTHER, HER SISTERS AND BROTHER

My mother, Pauline Bender, is second from left and seated among friends. Circa 1929, age 20.

Max Bender, 1938, age 31.

Thérese (Rési) Bender circa 1932, age 21.

Mimi Bender circa 1935, age 30.

MY FATHER, HIS SIBLINGS AND THEIR SPOUSES

Joseph [Schié] Gerstl in Switzerland 1939.

Paula Gerstl Gutstein, her husband David, and their daughter, Ruthe in Vienna 1937.

Left to right: Ludwig and Rosa Gerstl Holzer; Ernest Gerstl; Johanna Gerstl; Laura Gerstl Scharfberg; Hilda and Henry Gerstl. Photo circa 1949.

My father, William Gerstl, in Vienna 1936.

Author's Introduction

On a warm and sunny Sunday afternoon in 1988, while relaxing in my garden, I saw my father and mother in a different light. Perhaps it was the filtered rays of sunshine speckling their faces that revealed their signs of aging. My father was 84, and my mother 79. I had had plenty of opportunities to see the changes as the years passed, but I was too busy to think about it. My husband, Jerry, and I often saw my parents during the week, especially when we lived in Oak Park, Michigan, about one mile away from their home, and every Sunday was set aside for a planned activity that included both sets of parents. These routine Sunday afternoon rendezvous had started soon after our return from our honeymoon twenty-seven years earlier in 1961. As time went by, we unfortunately lost our parents, but when I started these interviews in 1988, only my father-in-law, William Olson, had passed away.

I had heard parts of "The Story," as I called my mother's tale of her Holocaust experiences, many times over the course of forty-some years. My mother would talk about it to anyone who would listen. She would cry, and that would annoy me, and my father as well. He often muttered under his breath, "Here she goes again," and would leave the room. He did not want to remember. It was over. He had a depressed disposition, perhaps because he internalized his suffering, and did not know how or wish to convey his feelings. I had picked up bits and pieces of "The Story" — segments that had made an impression on me and that I remembered — but everything was out of order and did not meld into a clear and comprehensible picture in my mind. I never attempted to make sense of it. There was just too much information, and it happened so long ago — 1938 to 1944. I just wasn't that interested. I had learned that I had saved my mother's life twice, but the information was vague because I never fully listened. Someday I would ask and make an effort to document the story from start to finish. It would flow smoothly, and I would be able to pass it on to my children, who in turn would pass it down to their children, and so on. But not right now. There was always something else to do that was more important.

On that warm and sunny Sunday afternoon, I saw the wrinkles and the tired eyes. We were having coffee in the garden and I suddenly felt an ache in my heart. It was fear, the realization that my mother and father were not immortal, and these blessed Sundays would someday come to an end. I felt panic. What if I missed the opportunity to get the complete story? It could happen. I realized that the time had come to pay attention.

Mom Olson was not with us that day. She had gone to Windsor, Canada, just across the border from Detroit, with Jerry's brother, Harvey, and his wife, Esther, to visit family. I hadn't planned to begin piecing the story together, but the ray of sunshine was my signal to start. I excused myself, went in the house, and got my tape recorder. This would be the beginning of many Sunday afternoons when I would avidly listen and record what my mother and father had to say. I was hungry to hear it all, eager to understand the whole story. I would find out what made my mother sigh so frequently, and why my father would sit alone in the living room, pensively staring into space without saying a word. To my surprise, on that sunny day, my father was willing to talk. I felt that he had read my mind.

It took more than a year to finish recording the story. I decided to name it *Maybe One Day* because it was a phrase frequently used by my father whenever he referred to developments he hoped for in the future. The next task was to translate numerous letters and documents that my mother had saved. She had official documents relating to the war years, personal documents, letters from her mother and brother, letters from our rescuers, photographs — a plethora of material relating to my parents' lives during WWII. Most moving were letters that my parents had written to each other while interned in separate detention camps. Everything was tattered and yellowed with age; after all, this written documentation had been stored in my father's briefcase for some fifty years. After my father died in 1993, Mom and I spent many afternoons translating it. Most was done, but unfortunately not all, before she died in 2006.

From 1988 until 2008, the tapes and translated material sat in a box. By 2008, we had already been blessed with six grandsons – Justin William Sachs, Jonah Lyndon Sachs, Aidan Lee Sachs, Maxwell Spencer Olson [Max], Joseph Isaac Olson [Joey], and Louis [Louie] Paul Light – and I became motivated to finish what I had started so long ago. The story had to be passed on, and it was my responsibility to do it. I retrieved my tape recorder and spent many hours at the computer, listening and transcribing the words of my cherished parents.

Our "bonus baby," another grandchild, came in 2009 — Jordin Cherna Lily Mechler — a year into my project. She carries my mother's Hebrew name "Cherna," and that of Lily Lasfargues, who, with her husband Emile, took care of me for more than a year when my parents had no choice but to give me up.

I look at my children and grandchildren and marvel at the fortunate outcome of "The Story." I have been telling it for some twelve years to schoolchildren visiting Michigan's Holocaust Memorial Center. I show copies of documents and photographs from my mother's archive as part of my presentation. One photo is of me wearing a gold chain with a cross around my neck that Lily and Emile made me wear to avoid suspicion from neighbors that I was Jewish. After speaking, I often get hugs from the children, and occasionally, I see tears from the adults who understand the deep sorrow and pain my parents must have felt in giving up their child, and the suffering that our family had to endure.

I end this introduction, as I end my presentation at the Holocaust Memorial Center, with these two questions: Would I have dared do what our rescuers did? What would you have done?

Jeannette Gerstl Olson

When Times Were Good

Vienna, 1933

Front row: My father, my Aunt Rėsi, a friend, and my mother. Standing in back are my mother's aunt and cousin.

Picnic on the Danube, 1932

Front row: My father wearing a white undershirt.
Back row: My mother wearing the dark bathing suit.

A SUMMARY OF OUR FAMILY'S SURVIVAL DURING WWII

Through the ages, Vienna, the capital of Austria, was one of the most beautiful and glamorous cities in the world. Its sophistication, culture, and elegance paralleled that of Paris. Historic monumental palaces and ornate architecture were evidence of its aristocratic past when emperors reigned. Vienna nurtured famous composers, artists, philosophers, architectural prodigies. It was the capital of sweets and music, producing, among others, such geniuses as Johann Strauss, father of the waltz, and Wolfgang Amadeus Mozart. World-renowned psychiatrist Sigmund Freud lived there, as well as Theodor Herzl, the visionary of Zionism that, many years later, led to the establishment of the State of Israel. Until its turbulent years under Hitler's barbaric rule in the 20th century, Vienna had a very large Jewish population that was a driving force behind the city's highly civilized culture. Jewish merchants, traders, entrepreneurs and businessmen contributed to its prosperity. In the field of medicine, three out of four Austrian Nobel Prize winners were Jewish, and more than half of Austria's physicians and dentists were Jews.

My mother, Pauline, the third child to my grandparents, Hermine and Sigmund Bender, was born into that Vienna on April 29, 1909. She was preceded by her sister, Wilhelmina [Mimi], then her brother, Max, and followed by Therese [Resi]. My grandparents, proprietors of a successful rope business, were affluent. They lived in a beautiful apartment in an upscale, non-Jewish neighborhood near the Park Schönbrunn, and owned a villa on the outskirts of Vienna in a town called Hinterbruhl, where they spent their summers. With the help of a housekeeper, my grandmother ran the household and took care of her family. The Bender children grew up in a musical home with a baby grand piano gracing the living room. Their friends would come over and

My mother at home, age 23.

gather around the piano to listen, sing and dance to music played by my grandmother or Mimi, both accomplished pianists. Occasionally, Max would accompany them on the violin, and Mimi would play the zither or the accordion.

As a young lady, my mother was chic and pretty, vivacious and full of fun. She loved city life with all its amenities. Outings with friends on the Danube shores, excursions to nearby small villages, picnics in nearby forests, trips to the mountains of St. Wolfgang, Salzkammergut, Salzburg, visits to museums, and concerts in the parks were among activities that filled her life. She attended a very fine school, and her future was promising. In 1926, when she was seventeen, my grandfather developed throat cancer, and her days of a carefree and untroubled existence came to an end. He did not have health insurance, and his medical expenses exceeded the savings that had been set aside to pay for health problems. The villa had to be sold and the money from the sale was deposited in a bank. Shortly after the sale of the villa, my grandfather died, the market crashed, and all the money was lost. The family suddenly found itself in dire financial difficulties. My mother had to drop out of school, take some secretarial courses, and get a job. In 1930, when she was twenty, she met my father, William Gerstl.

My father was born January 3, 1904, in Kobersdorf, Hungary, which later became part of Austria. His father, Samuel, died in 1907, age 39, when he collapsed while walking home from the synagogue on a Saturday morning. The cause of death was unknown, but the word was that it was related to an accident in his butcher shop a few days before. Sadly, he left his wife, Maria Johanna, a widow with seven young children: four sons, Joseph [Schié], Willy [three years old], Henry, and Ernst [one year old], and three daughters, Rosa, Paula, and Laura. As soon as they were old enough, the boys went to work to help support their mother and sisters. Circumstances did not allow my father the luxury of choosing a career. His vocation was assigned to him when a well-known tailor from Vienna came to Kobersdorf seeking an apprentice, and my grandmother was happy to accept an offer from him for her thirteen-year-old son. My father moved to Vienna, and received extensive training while working for this man. After formal examinations six years later, he earned diplomas with high distinctions in custom tailoring and pattern design. Fortunately, he had the talent and skill to succeed, and through the years, his work more than satisfied the most demanding and discriminating clientele.

Life was difficult and lonely for my father during his six-years of work and study. He missed his family. His teacher did not hesitate to hit him when not pleased with his work.

He was often hungry. There was an apartment building that he would pass on Wednesday deliveries, and one day he saw a loaf of bread on an outside window sill. He was so hungry that he took the bread and devoured it on the spot, not worrying about possible consequences. From that day on, every Wednesday when he passed the building, a bread would be waiting. He came to the conclusion that it was purposely left for him. He never found out who his benefactor was, but that charitable act was probably why, when times were better, he felt so strongly about helping others in need.

After leaving his apprenticeship, my father started his own business, and after a few years of being self-employed he went to work for the Kleiderhahn Custom Tailoring Company — a large and prominent custom tailoring firm. In 1937, he was promoted to an Associate position, and became chief cutter and pattern designer.

My father always dressed elegantly. Vienna 1926.

Business was good and his salary and benefits were excellent. He was a handsome, always well-dressed, serious, and pensive young man. He had not grown up in the carefree world of children, but was thrown into an adult world with responsibilities at a young age. At the onset of their romance, my mother was warned by my father's sisters that seeing him laugh was a rare event. They confided that "when he laughs, he laughs alone on the roof." Of course, my mother did not take that seriously, as he seemed to have no problem laughing in her presence, but later, after they married, she realized that there was some truth to their assessment of his disposition.

My parents met at a picnic on the banks of the Danube River while socializing with friends. Needing to use the facilities, my father excused himself and entered a restaurant nearby. A few minutes later, my mother and friends heard a crash of broken dishes followed by loud expletives and colorful language. When my father returned, visibly shaken and covered with food stains, he told my mother that in his haste to leave the restaurant, he had run into a waiter holding a huge tray full of dishes. My mother was certain that my father was so smitten by her good looks and personality that his mind was on her and not on his surroundings. I heard this story numerous times, and she always laughed when she told it. My father, characteristically, would do his best to pretend he saw no humor in it. He would try to keep a straight face, but his nostrils would flare and retract ever so slightly, his lips would quiver, and a couple of small snorts would slip out as he tried to stifle the urge to laugh. My mother, of course, would tease him mercilessly, and he would usually end up leaving the room.

My parents' courtship lasted five years. My father did not want to wed until his sisters had established homes of their own. My mother was willing to wait. After their wedding on April 28, 1935, life could have been good. They had family and friends, they lived in a wonderful city, and money was not an issue. Who would have thought that a population as sophisticated and cultured as the Viennese would become vicious,

bigoted, violent Nazi followers determined to destroy the Jews? An estimated 65,000 perished as a consequence of Austria's annexation with Adolph Hitler's Nazi Germany three years later in 1938. Lucky ones, including my parents, were able to flee at the expense of losing all their possessions and being exiled from their homeland. Many people wanted to escape, but neighboring countries had closed their borders and there was nowhere to go. The Holocaust was part of a war unlike any other, in which twelve million innocent people, not including soldiers and war casualties, perished in the most inhumane fashion imaginable. Six million were European Jews. Sadly, among the victims were many members of my mother's family, and most heartbreaking for her, her mother and her brother.

After their marriage in 1935, my parents settled in

My parents, April 28, 1935.

a nicely furnished apartment at Heinestrasse 3/8. My mother kept busy taking care of her home, and learning how to cook and keep a kosher kitchen, tutored by my father's mother. My father was doing well at Kleiderhahn. Three years later, they were not ready to have children because he wanted financial security before starting a family. Meanwhile, economic problems plagued Germany, and Adolph Hitler rose to power with grandiose plans to rebuild it into the world's most powerful country, populated exclusively by a pure and perfect Aryan race which would exclude the handicapped, homosexuals, gypsies, and Jews. Austria welcomed annexation with Nazi Germany, and cooperated with Hitler in his ferocious persecution of Jews. During the Night of Broken Glass [*Kristallnacht*] on November 9, 1938, Jewish neighborhoods were savagely attacked during organized riots throughout Germany and Austria. This event marked the beginning of the Holocaust.

My parents managed to flee Vienna at the end of December. My father's youngest brother, Ernst, and his wife, Grete, had entered Belgium illegally a few months earlier, and were safe in the city of Antwerp. Belgium had closed its borders as well, but it was possible to infiltrate by crossing a forest that was situated between Germany and Belgium. Ernst had informed my father of a guide who would, for a considerable sum of money, lead people across it. That strip of land was called "No Man's Land" because it belonged neither to Germany nor to Belgium, although it was patrolled by both countries. My father contacted this guide who instructed my parents to get a passport. He informed them that Jews were forbidden to take money or any of their belongings out of the country. They were restricted to one small piece of luggage per person. Everything they owned — their apartment, furniture, clothing, savings in the bank — would have to remain in Austria for the Germans. My father had a new leather briefcase in which he packed a little food, toiletries, documents, and a change of clothes. My mother had a backpack. They left Vienna and traveled by train across Germany to Köeln [Cologne], where they remained for about a week waiting for further instructions. They were housed by collaborators who were also well paid for their covert participation in the escape. On December 31, they met up with the guide and a group of twenty people, in Aachen, forty miles from Köeln, at the far west border of Germany. From that starting point, after passing a German checkpoint, the group walked through the night on a harrowing ten-hour trek across the forest.

They entered Belgium the next day, January 1, 1939, suffering from frostbite and exhaustion. They were told to wait in a barn while the guide went to get some taxis. My parents chose to be taken to Antwerp to join Ernst and Grete, Paula and her husband David, and their three-year-old daughter, Ruthe. Peace reigned for a while, and my parents had settled in. On Friday, May 10, 1940, Germany invaded Belgium, and all Jewish men from Austria and Germany were ordered to report to the police. My father and Ernst had to obey, and were immediately arrested. A few days later, in Brussels and in Antwerp, the men were marched to the trains, accompanied at gunpoint by Belgian soldiers, loaded into boxcars, and deported. My mother was devastated. She did not know where my father had been taken. She was left alone in her third month of pregnancy. My parents had been happy with the news that they were going to have a baby, but they knew that an invasion by the Nazis was forthcoming at any time. They decided to terminate the pregnancy. It made no sense to bring a child into the world when their lives were in peril and they would have to escape again. What chance did a pregnant woman have to survive the dangers that lay ahead? They learned of a nurse who could help with abortions, and my mother went to her home to seek her services. She did not have an appointment, and, fortunately for me, when she rang the doorbell no one answered. My mother believed this was meant to be, and decided to abandon her plan. She turned around and went home.

Now that my father had been deported, my mother and my Aunt Grete wanted to leave Belgium as soon as possible. They had been told that a transport of refugees was leaving by train from Antwerp on Tuesday, May 14th. France had allowed entry of 700,000 refugees from different countries, and this train with a capacity of 1800 was the last one going. My mother, Grete and her one-year-old daughter Cécile, and Grete's mother, boarded the train, unaware of its exact destination. A nightmarish three-day journey locked up in a boxcar under constant bombardment would take them to a refugee detention camp in the central southern part of France, Camp Frémont in Vallon-en-Sully.

My father and Ernst's journey from Antwerp took about two weeks until they arrived at their destination — a refugee detention camp for men in St. Cyprien, France, on the Mediterranean, close to the border of Spain. There had been a couple of brief stays at two other camps, one in Villeneuve and one in Villemur, but these were extremely overcrowded and could not hold additional internees. My father described Camp St. Cyprien "as big as a city." He saw countless rows of wooden barracks grouped into sections, each section surrounded by barbed wire. The barracks were flimsily built on sand and allowed little protection against wind, sand storms, cold, and rain. There were lice, insects, and disease, and a lack of proper nutrition, sanitation and medical care. About twenty-five hundred men waited apathetically for their turn to be loaded onto convoys of trucks that routinely came to deliver and pick up human cargo.

The two brothers spent about three months in St. Cyprien. They escaped after a camp authority, happy with the job my father had done altering one of his uniforms, warned him that both his and Ernst's names were on the next transport list to Gurs, one of France's worst transit stops on the way to the death camps. They decided that they had nothing to lose by running away, so they fled that night, escaping through an opening in the barbed wire. Because the security infrastructure was not as developed as in many of the camps in eastern Europe, escape was possible but extremely dangerous. People poorly dressed, lacking money, and not speaking the language were easily recognized as refugees and, if caught, faced harsh consequences and imprisonment in a French jail. My father and my uncle took that risk anyway, and escaped successfully. They ran along the sea in the night and arrived in Perpignan, about nine miles from Camp St. Cyprien. My father knew, through word of mouth in the camp, the approximate location of a hotel that housed an office of the underground. Its members were involved in secret activity to resist the apprehension of Jews and fight the Nazis. The two arrived at the hotel where they stayed for a couple of weeks while plans to travel to Nice were set in motion. During that time, a police officer who was a member of the organization asked my father to make him a suit. When the suit was finished, he offered to pay, but my father requested two Safe Transits instead, one for him and one for Ernst. These papers served as identification for non-Jewish immigrants, and gave the bearer legal rights to travel. Most importantly, they did not indicate religion. With these documents, my father and Ernst got on a train and traveled to Nice, where they met up with family members from Vienna who had settled there earlier.

The train cars taking my mother to Camp Frémont were crammed with people. These wagons were designated for transportation of coal, and contained absolutely no amenities for human comfort. Some people stood while others sat on the floor. They had to take turns. Lying down was impossible without infringing on someone's space. There were no roofs, and nights were cold. They traveled three days sustained only by the meager amount of food that they might have brought along for the trip, no water, no toilet facilities, wind and dust whipping around them, and enemy planes soaring overhead ready to drop bombs. Upon arrival in Vallon-en-Sully, these people were transferred into vehicles that took them to Camp Frémont. The camp was set up on the grounds of a lovely country estate that previously had been a private residence. My mother called it "a castle." The estate housed the commander of the camp and the guards. The three-hundred-some refugees were incarcerated in stables and barns and detained until deemed eligible for discharge.

The following month, June 1940, the French army was defeated by the Germans, and an armistice was signed. France agreed to relinquish its northern region, including Paris, to the Germans who would occupy it. The central and southern region would remain unoccupied, a Free Zone, but indirectly controlled by the Germans through Philippe Pétain, a French general who reached the distinction of Marshal of the Unoccupied [or Free] Zone, and was a Nazi collaborator. Vichy became the capitol of the unoccupied region, and its government under Pétain became known as the "Vichy regime." Many internment camps had been set up in the Free Zone where deportation or liberation was the policy, depending on the whim of the Pétain-appointed chief administrative official [Prefect] of the region.

At Camp Frémont, detention was to be temporary for refugees cleared of being a threat to France. Per strict German orders, however, German and Austrian Jews were excluded from liberation because the Germans had convinced the French that these interns were enemy aliens. A stipulation imposed by the Prefect of the region was that all pregnant women could be liberated after a confirmation of their condition by a military doctor. My mother was informed of this policy upon her arrival at Camp Frémont, and was anxiously awaiting freedom. Four months went by and her due date approached. She had not been seen by a doctor yet. She dreaded the possibility of having to deliver in the camp even though an Austrian medical student, also an internee, was prepared to help her. The problem was that the only available birthing instruments were dirty and rusty tools used for the horses that had once occupied the stalls. Three weeks before my birth, a physician was finally summoned and he confirmed her pregnancy. She was freed on September 26. At that time, the camp had been emptied except for sixty Austrian/German Jews who soon after were transferred to Gurs. My mother's pregnancy had saved her from that fate.

My parents had been able to correspond while in the camps. In September 1938, my father's brother, Henry, and his wife, Hilda, had escaped Austria and fled to Nice, France, a city on the coast of the Mediterranean. After they found a place to live, they sent my parents, who had not left Vienna yet, their address. In June 1940, after being incarcerated in their respective French detention camps, my mother wrote to them, letting them know where she was, as did my father, and so they found out through Hilda and Henry how to get in touch with each other. After what had seemed interminable worry, although they were still incarcerated, their spirits were lifted when they found out that each had survived. Thus correspondence between camps began. My father informed my mother about his plan to escape with Ernst to Nice, and she later received mail that they had arrived safely. When she was liberated, she sent him a telegram, and Hilda picked her up. My father could not risk traveling because he was a camp fugitive and would have been imprisoned had he been apprehended by the police. My parents were reunited on September 30th in Nice, and I was born on October 19th.

After a ten-day stay in the hospital, my mother and I went home to a room that my father had rented in an apartment on the Avenue Villermont that belonged to a single, elderly woman. They had kitchen privileges, and the laundry and diapers were washed in a sink and hung up to dry in the room. My Aunt Hilda and Uncle Henry lived in the same building one floor above. Not long after my father's arrival, he and Henry, who was also a tailor, rented a room in the building and used it as a workshop. They had a nice clientele and were able to make a living. They also got to know their neighbors, gentile people who would be instrumental in saving their lives later on. Food was scarce, as Germany depleted the country's supplies for its own needs. People queued up daily, food card in hand, for rations. The Nazis, occupying the north of France, were very close, and Jews in the Free Zone were uneasy and uncertain of their future.

Life went on as normally as possible until July 1942 when Marshal Pétain cooperated with the Nazis' demand of a higher quota of deportations of Jewish refugees from the Free Zone. A ghetto was setup in Nice, and the refugees were ordered to evacuate their homes and move into the ghetto to facilitate arrests. We were assigned a room in an old run-down hotel, the Hotel Pompeia. A systematic roundup was initiated by the Gestapo and the French police. Door-to-door searches and random arrests in the streets led to the deportation of thousands. Fortunately for my mother, women with children under the age of three were exempt for the time being, as were people over sixty. I would be two in October. My sixty-six-year-old paternal grandmother moved in with my mother and me in the Hotel Pompeai, while my father and my aunts and uncles went into hiding in the homes of the Christian families who had befriended them on Avenue Villermont. These people came to their rescue, risking their lives with that act of compassion.

The police went to the Hotel Ric Rac were Grete and Cécile were staying, and arrested them in the middle of the night because Cécile was three. They were taken to the police station, awaiting transport to Drancy, the main transit camp run by the Paris police force, from which 63,000 people were sent to their death in Auschwitz. The next morning, my mother realized that Cécile might not be considered Austrian because she was born in Belgium, and with proof, might be released. She urged Ernst to have someone take her birth certificate to the authorities. This was done, and Cécile was discharged. Grete was not so fortunate; she was among hundreds of captured refugees who were eventually taken to Auschwitz and murdered in the gas chambers. Ernst had begged her the day before her capture to bring Cécile and sleep in a cemetery with him, but due to an unfortunate printing error by the Jewish Committee which had announced that women and their children five years old [it should have been three] and older were being arrested, Grete felt safe and had refused. In November, the Germans came in full force into the Free Zone. They were now in control of the entire country, except for a small section in the southeastern region that was controlled by their ally, Italy.

My father and his family remained hidden until February 1943, when, with Germany's consent, the Italians took charge of the refugees. We were ordered to move to Vence, a small village a few miles away from Nice, in the Maritime Alps, under penalty of arrest if my parents did not obey. Under the Italians, it was now safe for my father to come out of hiding, and the three of us got on a bus and traveled to Vence. Although the Italians collaborated with the Germans, they were fairly nice and we were not mistreated. They disliked the Nazis, did not agree with their inhumane treatment of Jews, and refused to participate in the genocide that was going on. We were now in a different type of ghetto, being under surveillance at all times, but without the fear of imminent deportation. We had to report to headquarters twice a day, and were under house arrest from 7 o'clock at night until 7 o'clock in the morning. During the day, we were free to do as we pleased. There were occasional searches in refugee homes for possession of radios, newspapers, and weapons, which were forbidden. Men were allowed to work, and my father had the good fortune to meet Eugene Francone who owned a men's clothing store and needed a tailor. My father was hired and worked for him until August 30th. At that time, Germany, unhappy with the benevolence of the Italians towards the refugees, took over their territory, and ousted them out of France and back to Italy. They were ordered to take the refugees with them, and transport them to a detention camp near the Italian border by way of Nice. My father did not trust this situation, and made the decision to escape before the evacuation of the Italians. Without saying a word to anyone, including Mr. Francone, we got on a train in the middle of the night on August 30th, and fled to Nice where we had to go into hiding immediately. My father's premonition had been correct. The Jews who left with the Italian army walked straight into the hands of the Nazis who had invaded Nice. These unfortunate people, caught off-guard, were captured and deported to death camps.

When my parents arrived in Nice, they went directly to the Hotel Pertinax where my Aunt Hilda and Uncle Henry had been living. We could not stay there long, so Hilda took us to the home of gentile friends who were away on vacation for a week. She had the key to the apartment because she was watering their plants. We were desperate to find another hiding place as the owners would be back soon, but where? The Germans had become very aggressive in their search for German and Austrian Jews who had fled from Belgium, and our rescuers had to be extremely careful. It was very risky to hide a family with a young, noisy child — footsteps could be heard, and open windows could carry my voice to neighbors who might betray us. We were moved to an empty, hot and unkempt apartment that belonged to a grocer, Mr. Gineroli. After a while, it was decided that it would be safer for everyone if I were hidden separately from my parents. I was placed with a family who had previously hidden my father, and my parents were moved into a cave beneath Mr. Gineroli's grocery store.

Conditions in the cave were unfit for a prolonged stay. After six weeks of sleeping on wooden boards, having lost hope that this nightmare would soon end, weak from hunger, and tormented by the possibility that they might die, my parents decided it was time to find a permanent and secure home for me. They asked Mr. Gineroli to contact a childless couple who had volunteered to take me months earlier. At that time, my parents had refused, not wanting a long-term separation from their child. Now there was no choice. The couple, Emile and Lily Lasfargues, was notified, and Emile picked me up from the home where I was hidden. Once more I was removed from a place that had become familiar, and was taken to another town and a new home with strangers. My first childhood recollections are of my new "parents", Lily and Emile in Antibes, when I was three. I remember being happy with them and feeling loved, so much so that I forgot my mother and father.

Meanwhile, my parents were running out of money to pay Mr. Gineroli the small amount he needed for their keep. They sent a postcard to Mr. Francone in Vence disclosing their address, and asked if he would be interested in purchasing their leather briefcase, the only item they owned of some value. Upon receipt of the postcard, Mr. Francone went to Nice to fetch my parents and took them back to Vence that was still unoccupied. Not long after, the Nazis invaded Vence, at which time my parents had to hide again. Delphin and Antoinette Picco, Mr. Francone's in-laws took them in, risking deportation and death for sheltering Jews. My parents remained there until September 6, 1944, after the liberation of France by the Allied Forces. Once free, they went to Antibes to pick me up. Separation from Lily, who was now a widow, was very difficult for both of us. I was four years old and had believed, understandably, that she was my mother. I had to leave her and return to live with my parents. I had forgotten the German I spoke prior to moving in with Lily and Emile, but my mother had learned a little French in school that enabled us to communicate, albeit with difficulty. My parents were very anxious to leave Vence and start a new life in a bigger city. There was no future for us in that small village. We were the only Jews and my parents felt uncomfortable. Because Mr. Francone's business was booming, and my father's skills were a keystone to its success, my parents were reluctant to leave, feeling indebted to him and his family for risking their lives and sacrificing so much for us. We stayed until 1947 when my father accepted a position in a large tailoring firm in Cannes. We lived there until 1951 when we finally obtained our long-awaited visas to the United States.

Maybe One Day is a narration of the interviews that I conducted with my parents in 1988, detailing the saga of their flight from the Nazis and miraculous survival as a result of their courage, luck, and the aid of the Christian families who protected us and risked their lives to save our family.

WWII TIMELINE RELATED TO "MAYBE ONE DAY"

March 12, 13, 1938 – Nazi troops enter Austria which has a population of 200,000 Jews mainly living in Vienna. Hitler announces the Anschluss (union) with Austria.

April 26, 1938 – Nazis order Jews to register wealth and property.

June 14, 1938 – Nazis order Jewish owned businesses to register.

July 23, 1938 – Nazis order Jews over age fifteen to apply for identity cards from the police, to be shown on demand by any police officer.

July 25, 1938 – Jewish doctors prohibited by law from practicing medicine.

August 17, 1938 – Nazis require Jewish women to add "Sarah" and men to add "Israel" to their names on all legal documents, including passports, for identification of religious affiliation.

October 5, 1938 – Law requires Jewish passports to be stamped with a large red "J."

November 7, 1938 – Ernst Von Rath, secretary in the German Embassy in Paris, is shot and killed by Herschel Grynszpan, the seventeen-year-old son of one of the deported Polish Jews. Rath dies on November 9, precipitating Kristallnacht.

November 9, 10, 1938 – Kristallnacht [Night of Broken Glass.]

November 12, 1938 – Nazis fine Jews one billion marks for damages related to Kristallnacht.

November 15, 1938 – Jewish pupils are expelled from all non-Jewish German schools.

December 3, 1938 – Law for compulsory Arynanization of all Jewish businesses.

December 31, 1938/January 1, 1939 – My parents, William and Pauline Gerstl, cross a forest at night to flee Austria.

January 1, 1939 – My parents arrive in Belgium.

May 10, 1939 – My cousin Cécile Gerstl is born in Antwerp, Belgium.

September 3, 1939 – England and France declare war on Germany.

May 10, 1940 – Nazis invade Belgium, France, Holland, Luxembourg. Male Jewish refugees, including my father and my Uncle Ernst, are arrested.

May 11, 1940 – Male Jewish refugees, including my father and Ernst, are deported from Belgium.

May 14, 1940 – My mother leaves Belgium on a transport to France.

May 17, 1940 – My mother arrives at Camp Frémont, Vallon-en-Slly, France, and is incarcerated.

May 29, 1940 – My father arrives at Camp St. Cyprien, Basses-Pyrénés, France, and is incarcerated.

June 14, 1940 – France surrenders to Germany.

June 22, 1940 – Marshal Philippe Pétain signs an armistice with Hitler dividing France into an Occupied Zone with Paris as its capitol, and a Free Zone with Vichy as the capitol.

July 17, 1940 – The first anti-Jewish measures are taken in Vichy, France.

August 30, 1940 – My father escapes St. Cyprien and arrives in Nice middle of September.

September 26, 1940 – My mother is liberated from Camp Frémont and arrives in Nice four days later.

October 19, 1940 – I am born.

May 16, 1941 – French Marshal Philippe Pétain issues a radio broadcast from Vichy, France, approving collaboration with Hitler.

December 3, 1941 – My grandmother and my mother's brother, Max, are transported from Vienna to Riga, Latvia, where they are murdered by SS Einsatzgruppe A.

December 7, 1941 – Pearl Harbor is attacked by Japan. United States joins England and Russia, against the Axis Powers, Germany/Italy/Japan.

January 31, 1942 – SS Einsatzgruppe A reports a tally of 229,052 Jews killed.

July 1942 – Jews in Nice are moved into a ghetto. Roundup of all Jews begins in southern France by French police and Gestapo. Women with children under two are safe from deportation.

August 1942 – My father goes into hiding until February 1943.

November 11, 1942 – Italians and Germans invade Free Zone.

February 23, 1943 – My parents and other Jewish refugees are forced, by the Italians, to move and reside in Vence under their supervision.

August 30, 1943 – The Italians have surrendered to the Allied Forces, Nazi Germany orders Italy out of southern France and take over the region. Sensing life-threatening danger, we flee Vence and go back into hiding in Nice.

September 8, 1943 – The Italians leave Vence and are ordered by Germany to take the refugees with them to another detention camp.

September 1943 – I am moved to Antibes to live with Lily and Emile Lasfargues. My parents hide in a wine cellar in Nice.

December 1943 – My parents return to Vence where they are taken in by Antoinette and Delphin Picco, and hidden in their attic room until the liberation of France in August 1944.

June 6, 1944 – United States invades Normandy: D-Day.

August 15, 1944 – The south of France, including Vence, is liberated. My parents have to remain in hiding.

September 16, 1944 – My parents are free to leave their hiding place.

November 1944 – I am returned to my parents.

November 13, 1951 – We leave France.

November 27, 1951 – We arrive in New York.

When Times Were Good

Fun on the Blue Danube pre-war, 1931. My mother is seated in the back wearing a black bathing suit.

Hitler entering Vienna, 1938.

Source: "The History Place," Triumph of Hitler: Nazis Take Austria.

CHAPTER I

Vienna 1938

JO: When we came to Detroit in 1951, I was eleven years old. Seven years had passed since the defeat of Germany in France, and your liberation. You had gone through hell hiding from the Nazis. After we arrived, we lived in an upstairs flat, and Tante Paula, Uncle David and Ruthe lived downstairs. We were safe in the United States, yet I remember how often you would cry. Why were you so unhappy?

Ma: My nerves were shot. I didn't know what happened to my family. We had no money. We had brought $300 — that's all we had been able to save — and immediately had to give $150 of it to our landlord to cover painting expenses after the former tenants had left. We needed every penny to live on — who cared about painted walls! Had we stayed in New York like I wanted to, we would have gotten help from a Jewish organization that helped the "Greenhorns" — that's what the American Jews called the newcomers. I was insulted by that name. Because we came to Detroit and had family here, we were rejected and had to fend for ourselves. Someone had made an announcement at a local synagogue that we were poor refugees and needed help, so people who had had the good fortune of avoiding the war gave us their rejects. They were refurbishing their homes and we got the discards. You probably think that we should have been grateful, but we were still the same people inside as we had been in our former life, and this shamed and humiliated us. I was so angry at Papa for not wanting to stay in New York.

Pop: I hated New York, it was so noisy and crazy, I couldn't wait to leave. Besides, I had my sister, Paula, in Detroit, and I wanted to be with her. When we got here, I was hired to do alterations and earned next to nothing. I was so sorry that we hadn't returned to Vienna. That's what I had wanted to do. I knew the country, I spoke the language, I had family … But Ma refused.

JO: But you did find a good job at Lieber and Son.

Pop: Yes. Eventually, I was hired in the field that I was trained for, so that was good, but the pay was not that great. Ma had to go to work so that we could save some money, and I wasn't happy about that. I did stay with Lieber over thirty years, until I retired.

JO: I remember occasionally being invited for dinner by friends of Tante Paula and Uncle David. Ma, you would start talking about the war. Unfortunately, they didn't want to hear about it; they wanted to talk about pleasant things.

Ma: Hitler was able to brainwash an entire population. He got away with slaughtering millions of people, including my family, and nations were indifferent. It's hard to believe that this barbarism happened, and you can imagine how I felt when our own people here, in the United States, were indifferent as I spoke.

Pop: I just wanted to forget it.

Ma: It made me feel better to talk about it. People would shut me up by saying, "You weren't the only ones who suffered. We had to go through the Depression." That would make me so mad. Can you imagine comparing the Depression to the fate of the Jews during the Holocaust? Being hunted down for years, fearing for our lives, losing family and friends, being tortured, death through murder, disease and starvation? It wasn't enough that we went through those horrible times; we had no sympathy or psychological support from anyone here.

JO: During my childhood and teenage years, so often you used to sigh with a simultaneous, whispered "Ah ya." I would talk to you but your eyes were vacant and I could see that you were not hearing what I was saying. Your mind was turned inwards concentrating on images that I couldn't see.

Ma: Yes, I couldn't stop thinking about what happened to my mother and my brother, my aunts and uncles, my cousins. There was no word. I was enraged by the evil we had lived through. I worried about when we would finally be able to go to the United States. We lived from day to day not knowing where our future would take us. You were our joy, but we were always nervous and stressed and I'm not surprised that you felt it.

JO: You were loving parents and made sure that I had everything I needed. Although it pained me to see you unhappy, I grew up feeling very secure. I did listen to you when you talked about the war, but I never heard the story in sequence from beginning to end, and today is a good time to begin. O.K.?

Pop: O.K.

JO: How old were you when your life turned upside down because of Hitler?

Pop: I was thirty-four years old and Ma was twenty-nine. We were married almost four years.

JO: Do you remember when the Germans came into Vienna?

Pop: Not much. I was not home. Maybe I was at work.

Ma: I remember everything like it was yesterday.

Pop: Sometimes I just have to hear a few words, and all of a sudden things come back.

JO: You married in 1935. Austria was not involved with Germany yet. Did you experience any anti-Semitism at that time?

Ma: No. Vienna was a wonderful city, and we enjoyed everything it had to offer. We had many friends, Jewish and non-Jewish. We had a permanent lease on a beautiful apartment.

Pop: Heinestrasse 3, on the third floor.

Ma: Yes, it was in the first district, a very nice Jewish neighborhood. The building had about six floors. The outside was very ornate, as were most buildings in Vienna, with shapes and figures protruding from the concrete walls. It was situated on a wide, tree-lined boulevard. We were walking distance from lovely stores.

JO: What do you mean by a permanent lease?

Ma: Our contract could not be terminated. We had the right to live there as long as we wanted and we could remodel and change things. We updated the kitchen "modern American" style immediately after we moved in. I loved it. Our furniture was custom-made and we had beautiful accessories that we had received as wedding gifts and that we had bought. Papa had a well-paying position as chief cutter and pattern designer for the Kleiderhahn Custom Tailoring Company, and he had been promoted as an associate of the firm. He also did some custom tailoring at home. One of our rooms was a reception area for his clients. Everything looked rosy at that time. It was so nice and we were very happy.

JO: Did you work?

Ma: No. Papa made a nice living and I didn't have to work. He actually didn't want me to work. I was busy taking care of our apartment and doing the grocery shopping every day. I would go to Mémé's [my paternal grandmother] house a couple times a week, and she would teach me how to cook and keep kosher. I made my own clothes, I got together with friends, we went out a lot with other couples … it was a normal life.

JO: When did things change?

Ma: When Hitler and his troops rolled into Austria in March 1938, and announced the Anschluss [union] of Austria and Germany. He arrived in Vienna on April 2, 1938.

JO: Did you see this?

Ma: No, but I saw the troops parading down our street more than once. They would march and sing Nazi songs. We Jews were forbidden to be in the streets during their parading, nor could we be seen looking out a window or from a balcony. I would go to a neighbor's apartment because she faced the main street, and we would look from behind her curtains. Buildings were being watched. Anyone spotted looking out could have been shot.

JO: Why?

Ma: There were dissidents and the Nazis wanted to make sure that no one would attempt to shoot Hitler or his troops.

JO: Describe what you saw during these marches.

Ma: Tens of thousands of people, waving Nazi flags, arms extended in the Sieg Heil salute [*Hail to Victory*], throwing flowers and confetti at the feet of the troops. The annexation was nicknamed the Blumenkrieg [*The War of Flowers*].

JO: Sounds like the masses were happy.

Ma: They welcomed the Nazis with open arms. They were overjoyed to be part of the Deutsches Reich [*German Empire*] with Hitler as their leader.

JO: When did Hitler appoint himself Chancellor of Austria?

Ma: After the election on April 10, 1938. Jews did not take part in this election because they had been stripped of their right to vote and their citizenship. Dr. Kurt von Schuschnigg had been Chancellor since 1934, and we were sure that he would be re-elected and things would get better. He was against the Anschluss. Anyway, he was forced to resign before the election. The ballot consisted of one option: to approve the Anschluss and a totally Nazi Parliament — yes or no. Ninety nine percent voted yes. It was set up so Hitler would win, and we were not prepared for this.

JO: What happened after the annexation?

Ma: The next day, at 7:30 in the morning, there was a knock at the door. It was one of the cutters who worked with Papa, Mr. Straggi. I asked him, "Mr. Straggi, what are you doing here so early?" He said, "Don't you know what's going on?" I said no, trying to be as expressionless as possible. He wanted to see our reaction to the new regime, and I didn't want to give him the satisfaction of seeing us the least bit worried or afraid. He put up his arm bearing the swastika to let us know that he was a member of the Party. We had been very good friends until then, and often had socialized with him and his wife. On his way out, he said, "Things are going to be very dangerous for the Jews." He left, and after that, we didn't associate with him anymore. A couple of hours later that day, there was banging at our door. I asked, "Who is it?" We had a little peephole and I saw a hand covering it. I heard a male voice yelling, "Mache die Tur auf." [*Open the door.*] I didn't open right away, so the voice yelled again, "Mach sie auf!" [*Open it up!*] I opened it and there stood five or six Gestapos in full uniform, guns and all. I was terrified. They told me to get a broom and "Komm mit!" [*Come along!*]

JO: How old were they?

Ma: They were young, maybe late teens or early twenties. Papa was not home. I obeyed and joined a crowd of people standing outside holding brooms and mops. I was ordered to start walking with them from house to house, picking up other Jews. Finally, we arrived at the NordWestBahn Halle, a train station in Vienna. It was dirty and littered with debris. We were told to clean it up and make beds. I worked until four in the afternoon. I was exhausted. Photographers came and took pictures.

JO: There were beds in the station?

Ma: Yes, for Hitler's soldiers. While sweeping, I found a wallet. I gave it to a German soldier, and he said, "You are very honest. I'll see if you can go home." He had to get permission from a superior to dismiss me, but the request was denied, and I had to stay and continue sweeping.

When I got home, Papa was frantic. He didn't know where I was taken, or if I was coming back. Every day we would hear many stories about Jews getting beaten up, jailed, terminated from their jobs, losing their businesses, and disappearing. We would hear screaming in the streets, even gunshots. People were afraid to leave their homes. Walking the streets was dangerous. Many applied for visas to other countries, and were successful in fleeing Austria. In February 1939, after a brief stay in Belgium, Tante Paula, Uncle David and their three-year-old daughter, Ruthie, left for the United States.

JO: Why couldn't you leave too?

Ma: There was a strict immigration quota. You had to have a sponsor in the United States who would sign that he or she had enough funds to be financially responsible for the applicants, should the need arise, so they would not become a burden to the country. David had a brother in California who sponsored the three of them, and was able to send affidavits. They were lucky to leave when they did because the Nazis invaded Belgium shortly after. I loved Ruthie so much. I felt that I could never love another child as much, not even my own, until you were born. Then you became the world to me. We were very sad when they left, but it saved their lives. In 1942, the Nazis started rounding up German and Austrian Jews in the south of France where we lived. They did this in a very organized, calculated, and systematic manner,,,from apprehension to extermination…all Jews, in due time. Ruthie was born in Vienna and would have been about six years old in 1943. She and Tante Paula probably would have been taken to Drancy and perished in Auschwitz, as did Tante Grete. They would have fit in the "women with children over the age of three" deportation category, and I highly doubt that they would have survived.

JO: What happened after Kristallnacht?

Ma: One Sunday, we were walking to our friends' house. A husky young boy riding a bicycle came towards us, went to Papa and said, "Komm mit!" Papa had no choice but to go with him. I had no idea where he was being taken. I was so frightened, and I didn't know what to do. I didn't want to be alone, so I went to Mémé's house. A few hours later, Papa came back. He had been taken to a junkyard where men were sorting pieces of steel and loading them into a truck. Papa was a cutter and used his hands for his trade. An injury would have jeopardized his ability to work. Fortunately, he was not hurt.

Pop: When I got there, the truck was almost full. I worked for a while, and then I was allowed to leave.

Ma: The Nazis started searching Jewish homes looking for weapons. If anything was found, the item was confiscated and the people were deported. I had taken fencing lessons and had a complete fencing outfit, including the helmet and the sword. I gave it to my mother who lived in the outskirts of Vienna in a non-Jewish area. She took it to a ditch, and threw it all in. My mother wasn't afraid of anything. She was a very brave woman. She refused to leave Vienna, and eventually perished at the hands of the Nazis.

JO: When did this happen?

Ma: In 1941 when all the remaining Jews in Vienna were rounded up.

JO: I don't want to digress from 1938. We have to follow the timeline, so let's return to Vienna at the beginning of the Nazi takeover.

Voting ballot from April 10, 1938. Anschluss, *Wikipedia.org*

Do you agree with the reunification of Austria with the German Empire that was enacted on March 13, 1938, and do you vote for the party of our leader, Adolph Hitler?

Large circle labeled "Yes" — Small circle labeled "No"

Kristallnacht, November 1938

Jews arrested during Kristallnacht line up for roll call at the Buchenwald concentration camp.
Lorenz C. Schmuhl Papers, USHMM Archives.

CHAPTER II

Kristallnacht (Night of Broken Glass)

Ma: In May 1938, a couple of months after the Anschluss, the Nazis ordered all Jews who lived in small towns and villages to evacuate their homes and move to Vienna. Papa had an aunt and uncle who were also Gerstls. They lived in Kobersdorf where Papa was born, a small town close to the Hungarian border. They had six children ranging in age from three to eleven. When they arrived, we had to find housing for all of them, but no one had a dwelling spacious enough to keep the family together. Hilda and Henry found a room for the parents, and took in Lisl who was the oldest. The remaining children were housed among various family members. Papa and I took one of their daughters, Ruthi, who was six years old. We were not considering leaving Vienna yet, even though an exodus had begun.

JO: When was Kristallnacht?

Ma: November 9, 1938. Throughout Germany and Austria, Jewish neighborhoods were brutally attacked by the Nazis. It was a planned night of violence triggered in Paris by a Jewish young man who killed a German officer because his parents had been taken to a concentration camp. The streets were covered with so much glass from broken windows that this violent night became known as "Kristallnacht" — Crystal Night — better known as "The Night of Broken Glass."

JO: Were you directly affected by it?

Ma: Oh yes. We were awakened by screams in our apartment building. I ran to the stairwell, and saw a gang of what looked like teenage boys wearing Nazi uniforms running up the stairs carrying axes and sledgehammers. They smashed down doors, destroyed whatever they could get their hands on, and dragged people out. Below us lived an Orthodox rabbi and his family. We thought that they had killed all of them. I can't describe the terror we felt hearing blows and screams in the building. There was no escape from our apartment, and we were helplessly waiting to be next. Somehow the caretaker was able to get them out before they reached our floor and we were not hurt. I won't ever forget that night. Meanwhile, we were relieved to hear the next day that the rabbi and his family had fled to Egypt a few days before.

JO: What did you see the next day?

Pop: There was destruction everywhere. Streets were littered with broken furniture, glass, and stuff from people's apartments. There was smoke from buildings that had been burned down, including synagogues and holy books. There were mass arrests by the Gestapo, and thousands of Jewish men were deported to extermination and work camps. Many people were killed.

Ma: Do you remember my Uncle Max Lindenfeld? We stayed at his apartment in New York when we came to the United States.

JO: Of course I remember him. We lived with him for ten days in December 1951 before moving to Detroit. He was old and had a terribly depressing apartment in Manhattan.

Ma: He and his wife, Mathilde, had a son, Kurt, who was about twenty and lived at home with his parents on Josefinagasse. About a week after Kristallnacht, the SS came to their apartment and arrested him. They were looking for doctors, and Kurt's brother, Irwin, was a doctor. He was the one they had come for. Irwin, however, had already left for Argentina, so they took Kurt. A few weeks later, an SS officer came knocking at the door to inform Max and Mathilde that Kurt was shot to death on the train to Dachau. The man had a box with him and he wanted to sell it to my aunt and uncle for 10,000 schillings, telling them that it contained their son's ashes. Can you imagine how evil he was? They refused.

JO: Why?

Ma: How could they know that these ashes were, in fact, their son's? They could have been the ashes of a cremated animal or of another person. Anyone as evil and heartless as this boor standing in their apartment was probably also a liar.

JO: You mention the SS. Who were they?

Ma: They started out as a group of bodyguards for Hitler and his officers. During WWII, it grew into a huge organization that became a part of the government. Their job was to exterminate all Jews. Members of the SS were known for their cruelty and ferocity, and were responsible for carrying out the killing, torture, and enslavement of approximately twelve million people, including six million Jews during the Holocaust.

JO: What did you do the day after Kristallnacht?

Pop: We were afraid to stay in our apartment. What if this happened again? Ruthi still lived with us. The three of us got into a taxi and went to Hetzendorf where Ma's mother lived. It was a gentile area and there were no disturbances there, so we stayed a few days until things calmed down. On the way there, I remember seeing six or seven priests coming out of a church. While going down the steps, they were shot by Nazi soldiers. I saw that.

JO: Priests?

Pop: Priests.

JO: Why would they shoot priests?

Pop: I don't know. Maybe they opposed the regime and helped the victims.

JO: What finally convinced you to leave Austria?

Pop: A warning from a member of the Nazi Party.

JO: How did you know a member of the Nazi party?

Pop: The owner of the store where I worked, Mr. Hahn, and his two sons-in-law, Pollack and Weiss, were Jewish. There were eighteen Jewish employees. I had been promoted as an associate of the firm. As soon as the Nazis came into Austria in March, Jews were fired from their jobs and they were replaced by "Aryan" workers. The Jews were given low-paying jobs, work that entailed menial tasks like cleaning streets, collecting garbage, etc.

Ma: My brother, Max, was an accountant. He was let go and forced to work outside on the railroad tracks. It was difficult labor, especially for someone who was not strong. He was hurt in the process. I have letters from him and my mother where they talk about an injury to his leg. He was hospitalized a couple of times because of that. He made light of it in his letters because they were censored. He could have gotten in trouble if he revealed too much.

Pop: Jewish businesses were taken away from the owners. Hahn was thrown out and the store was sold to an Aryan. His name was Thomas Krabath. The Nazis put Pollack in a cart with a sign hanging from his neck saying "Jewish Profiteer," and paraded him around neighboring streets. This was to build up hatred against Jews by accusing them of taking financial advantage of people. This, of course, was not true. The Kleiderhahn Company paid union wages, and everything was done correctly; it was simply propaganda.

All of Kleiderhahn's Jewish employees were fired except the store manager, Neue, and me because we were needed to train the new Aryan personnel. A relative of Krabath, his name was Franz Podzimek, was administrator of the Commissariat, a position in the SS. He would tell us that he was only wearing the Nazi uniform but he was not a Nazi. He informed us that Jews were in a lot of danger, but reassured us that nothing would happen to us because we were needed in the store. On July 1, 1938, four months before Kristallnacht, he gave Neue and me an official letter with orders that we not be arrested. Once, on my way home, I was crossing a bridge, and someone stopped me. "Jew?" he said, and I said, "Yes." "Komm mit!" At that point, I showed him the letter, and he let me go. Podzimek told me that at police headquarters there was a huge stack of files identifying the Jewish men to be arrested. As our files moved up, he would move them back to the bottom. In September, he came to the store and told us that he could no longer do that because the stack was too small. He couldn't help us anymore, and he informed us that if we wanted to live, it was time that "we disappear."

Historical Information
The Aryanization Process

Aryanization referred to the forced transfer of Jewish-owned businesses to German "Aryan" ownership. The Aryanization process had two stages: the so-called "voluntary" stage, from which Jews were excluded from German economic life, and the compulsory stage that began immediately after Kristallnacht. In this final stage, all Jewish-owned businesses that had not already been "Aryanized" were liquidated within a few weeks and transferred to a government trustee. Jews who fled were forced to "donate" their remaining property to the state.

The Association of 'German' Aryan Clothing Manufacturers was established in Berlin under the Reich Ministry of Economy to direct the Aryanization of the fashion industry. The ADEFA label in German clothing guaranteed the buyer that the garment had been manufactured "by Aryan hands only."

Ironically, Magda Goebbels and Emmy Goring, wives of highly placed Nazi officials, continued to buy from their favorite Jewish designers until official Aryanization in the late 1930s made it impossible. Even after Aryanization had begun, the Nazis placed orders for uniforms with Jewish manufacturers. By 1939, however, all areas of clothing manufacture were "Judenrein" — free of Jews.

Jews received little or no compensation in the expropriation of their property and businesses. Even after the war, most of these forced transfers were not overturned or compensated.

Source: *Answers.com*

My father, far left, and colleagues at Heinrich Hahn's "Kleiderhahn Custom Tailoring Company" in 1937. Patterns were custom designed and cut by my father. Together with his colleagues, the garments were completed.

KLEIDERHAHN
H. HAHN
POSTSPARKASSENKONTO NR. 148.468
TELEGR.-ADR.: KLEIDHAHN
GIRO-KONTI:
OESTERR. CREDIT-ANSTALT—
WR. BANKVEREIN, WIEN, XIV.

Wien, am ....1....Juli.....1938.

XIV., Sparkasseplatz 6, Telefone: R-39-0-45, R-39-0-46
VI., Mariahilferstr. 47, Telefon:

B E S T A E T I G U N G

Ich, Pg. Franz P o d z i m e k, kommissarischer Verwalter (lt. Be - stätigung des Staatskommissaers f.d. Privatwirtschaft) der Firma: "Kleiderhahn", Wien XIV.Sparkassaplatz 2, bestätige hiermit, dass ich Herrn Wilhelm G e r s t l, Zuschneider der Firma H.Hahn, ("Kleiderhahn") zur Arisierung der Firma, welche im vollen Gange ist, unbedingt benötige, sowie es auch im Interesse der arischen Angestellten und auch des neuen arischen Betriebsführers gelegen ist. Zur Einschulung bezw. Neueinführung benötige ich Genannten dringend und möge daher von Verhaftungen oder dergl. bis zur endgültigen Durchführung der Arisierung der Firma abgesehen werden.

Der kommissarische Verwalter

S. Bl. Nr. 80/1938.

KLEIDERHAHN   Vienna, July 1, 1938
H. HAHN

CONFIRMATION

I, Franz Podzimek, Administrator of the Commissariat (as confirmed by the State Committee for Private Enterprises), for the company Kleiderhahn, Vienna, XIV. Sparkasseplatz 2, confirm herewith that Mr. Wilhelm Gerstl, cutter and tailor of the H. Hahn company (Kleiderhahn) is urgently needed during the Aryanization phase of the company, which is in full swing, as it is in the best interest of the new Aryan employees and Aryan management. As I crucially need the above-named for training and hiring new employees, I am requesting refraining from arresting him, etc., until the finalization of the company's Aryanization.

Administrator of the Commissariat
Franz Podzimek

KLEIDERHAHN

Wien, 13.Juli 1938.

Z e u g n i s

womit bestätigt wird, dass Herr Wilhelm Gerstl, Wien, II.,
Heinestrasse 3/8 wohnhaft, vom 18.September 1933 bis zum heutigen
Tage bei uns als erster Herren Mass-Zuschneider und Modelleur
auch für englische Damenmäntel und Kostüme zu unserer vollsten
Zufriedenheit tätig war.

Herrn Gerstl können wir ruhig als Meister in seinem Fach
bewerten, der es vorzüglich versteht, in gewinnender Art jedem
Wunsche auch der verwöhntesten Kunde vollauf gerecht zu werden.

Wegen Arisierung des Geschäftes wurde Herr Gerstl von
uns abgefertigt.

H. HAHN
(KLEIDERHAHN)
Wien XIV., Sparkassepl. 6

WIEN XIV SPARKASSEPLATZ 6

Document signed by Jewish owner, H. Hahn, stating that William Gerstl has been terminated due to Aryanization of the Kleiderhahn Company. Vienna, July 13, 1938

Vienna, July 13, 1938

This certificate confirms that Mr. William Gerstl, who resides in Vienna, II., Heinestrasse 3/8, has been employed by this company from September 18, 1933, until the present day, as senior custom pattern designer and cutter for men's apparel, as well as for English style ladies' coats and suits, to our fullest satisfaction.

We can confidently recommend Mr. Gerstl as Master in his profession, as he thoroughly understands and satisfies the wishes of the most discriminating customers.

Because of Aryanization of the company, we were obligated to terminate Mr. Gerstl.

H. HAHN
(KLEIDERHAHN)

KLEIDERHAHN
H. HAHN
POSTSPARKASSENKONTO NR. 148.488
TELEGR.-ADR.: KLEIDHAHN
GIRO-KONTI:
OESTERR. CREDIT-ANSTALT —
WR. BANKVEREIN, WIEN, XIV.

Wien, am 30. Juli 1938.
XIV., Sparkasseplatz 6, Telefone: R-39-0-45, R-39-0-46
VI., Mariahilferstr. 47, Telefon:

Wir bestätigen hiermit, dass Herr Wilhelm Gerstl, in unserer Firma bis zur Einarbeitung einer Ersatzperson mit Bewilligung des Wirtschaftsamtes des Kreises VII in Stellung ist.

THOMAS KRABATH
vormals
KLEIDERHAHN

This document is signed by Thomas Krabath, the new Aryan owner.

KLEIDERHAHN
   H. HAHN

Vienna, July 30, 1938

   With permission of the Reich Ministry of the Economy, we confirm, herewith, that Mr. William Gerstl is to remain employed by our company only until a replacement has been trained.

Thomas Krabath
Formerly KLEIDERHAHN
A German Aryan Enterprise

KLEIDERHAHN

Z e u g n i s

mit bestätigt wird, dass Herr Wilhelm G e r s t l,
geboren am 3. Jänner 1904, während der Zeit vom 18. September 1933
bis 23. September 1938 in meinem Hause als Zuschneider und Modelleur
zu meiner vollsten Zufriedenheit beschäftigt war. Der Genannte war
ein fleissiger und gewissenhafter Arbeiter, sodass ich ihn jedermann
aufs beste empfehlen kann.

Die Auflösung des Dienstverhältnisses erfolgte wegen Arisierung
des Betriebes.

THOMAS KRABATH
vormals
KLEIDERHAHN
Wien XIV. Sparkassepl. 6 u. 2
Tel. R 39-0-45 u. R 39-0-46
DEUTSCH ARISCHES UNTERNEHMEN

Wien, 23. September 1938.

Letter of recommendation from Thomas Krabath who gave my father one year's worth of salary as a parting gift.

This is to certify that Mr. William Gerstl, born on January 3, 1904, was employed in my establishment from September 18, 1933 until September 23, 1938, as cutter and pattern designer, to the fullest extent of my satisfaction. He was a diligent and knowledgeable worker, and I can recommend him as the best to anyone.

The termination of service was implemented due to Aryanization of the establishment.

Thomas Krabath
Formerly KLEIDERHAHN
Vienna XIV. Sparkassepl.6 u.2
A German Aryan Enterprise

Vienna, September 23, 1938

The Briefcase

Photo taken in 2013

CHAPTER III

The Briefcase 1938

JO: When Franz Podzimek told you that "it was time to disappear," were you surprised?

Pop: Not at all. I knew that it would happen eventually. Things were getting worse and worse for the Jews. Of course, we hoped that the Germans would get out of Austria, and life would return to normal, but we knew that this was unlikely to happen soon. Most of the family had already left. After Podzimek's warning, we had to consider our options.

JO: What were your options?

Pop: We didn't have many. Unoccupied countries had closed their borders. We were ready to go to Shanghai, but Ma's mother talked us out of it because it was so far. We wanted to go to America, but we didn't have a sponsor. We tried Australia and Argentina, but that didn't work out. Finally, Ernst and I made plans to join Schié, who had already fled to Switzerland. I bought a good, strong leather briefcase and packed a few necessities. The day before our departure, as fate would have it, all Jews were put under house arrest and we could not leave.

JO: Why were Ma and Grete not going with you?

Pop: At that time, the men were in danger of deportation. Ernst and I figured that we would be safe in Switzerland and our wives would eventually join us. We never dreamt that Hitler was planning a "Final Solution to the Jewish Problem," and Germany would become a killing machine.

Ma: It was a good thing that Papa did not go. He would not have been able to return, and I would not have been able to leave. Eventually I would have been deported along with my mother and my brother.

JO: So what did you do?

Ma: Our only option was to go to Belgium. Ernst's wife, Grete, had a sister, Lisl, who lived in Ostend, a seaside resort on the North Sea coast in northern Belgium. She had informed Grete how to get in illegally because legal entry was no longer possible. Germany and Belgium were separated by a forest known as "No Man's Land" because it did not belong to either country. It was a dangerous area closely patrolled by soldiers of both armies. Guided by someone who knew the way, it was possible to cross this forest from Aachen, a city in Germany near the Belgian border, and enter Belgium. Ernst and Grete,

Paula, David and their two-year-old daughter Ruthie, had taken that route in September 1938. Ernst wrote to us and referred us to a guide. We contacted him and made arrangements to join a group that he was taking in December. He charged a lot of money for this.

JO: What did he tell you to do in preparation for the trip?

Ma: We needed a passport and were restricted to one small piece of luggage each. Papa already had his briefcase, and I had a backpack. As far as money, we paid cash. Jews could leave the country but were forbidden to withdraw their money from the bank or take any of their belongings.

JO: What about your apartment?

Ma: Two Gestapos came by one day, looked around and ordered us to sell our furniture. We had no choice. They estimated the value at next to nothing and we lost a lot of money from that transaction. Luckily, we had heard that property belonging to Jews was being confiscated, so when they came, we had already taken our crystal, sewing machine, Papa's patterns, photo albums, and other items that were valuable and/or sentimental to us, to my mother who lived in a gentile area. As for our apartment and our savings in the bank, we were forced to leave it. Krabath had given Papa one year's worth of salary upon his dismissal, that's how much he liked him. We knew not to deposit the money in the bank, so we had a lot of cash.

Pop: In one day, I gave it all away. I gave most of it to Ma's mother, and some to family members who were not leaving Vienna.

JO: Who were the Gestapo?

Ma: The German secret police. They had the power to imprison people without any cause.

JO: When did you leave?

Ma: We left Vienna middle of December 1938, and crossed into Belgium the night of December 31st. It would be a long walk through the forest, so we were instructed by the guide to take only what we could carry. We packed all our documents, including birth certificates, diplomas, marriage license, etc. in the briefcase. We also took along some clothing, toiletries, and some food. We wanted to take little Ruthi with us, but were afraid to risk her life. Who knew what dangers awaited us. She had lived with us for seven months. Such a cute, sweet child. Her parents were still in Vienna, and we felt it would be better for her to remain with them. In the 1941 roundup of Jews in Vienna, she and her whole family, except for her brother, Egon, were sent to Dachau or Buchenwald — I am not sure which — where they perished. Egon somehow got out of Vienna alone at the age of 14, and ended up in what was then Palestine. I don't know his story. He married young, lived on a kibbutz, and had lots of children. I always regretted that we couldn't save his sister, Ruthi. We had to make decisions, just go with our instincts, and we felt that it would be too risky for her and for us.

JO: When did Franz Podzimek warn you to disappear and why didn't you leave right away?

Pop: He told me in July. It took that long for us to figure out what to do. We were the last ones in my family to leave Vienna.

Ma: Hilda and Henry, Mémé, Rosa and Ludwig left in November, and went directly to France.

JO: Did they end up in a camp like you did?

Ma: No, because they went through Italy. I don't know how they did it. They were luckier.

JO: Why didn't your mother and your brother, Max, go with you?

Ma: My mother did not want to leave because she felt that she was too old — she was sixty-nine. She also felt safe because she lived in a non-Jewish area. I don't think that she was totally aware of the dangers facing Jews. Had she been, she might have fled with us, or perhaps she might have convinced my brother, Max, to leave. We could not force her and felt that perhaps she was right. Max was 32 years old, engaged to a young woman, Marianne Robichek, who had fled to England. He did not want to leave my mother alone, so he stayed with her. When all Jews were fired from their jobs or lost their businesses, he was terminated from his position as an accountant. Because he had light hair and bluish eyes, he could pass for Christian. Somehow he was able to get a Swastika and by posing as an Aryan, he got a job as a salesman. This allowed him to support himself and my mother, until someone betrayed him. When his ruse was discovered, he was severely beaten and then was ordered to work on the railroad tracks. On November 30, 1941, he and my mother were picked up from their apartment in Hetzendorf by the Gestapo, and were taken to a ghetto in Vienna, where they stayed until deportation. [*Mom is holding back tears.*]

JO: Can you go on?

Ma: Yes.

JO: How did you get this information?

Ma: We were able to get mail from them while we were incarcerated in the detention camps, and later in Nice. I have Max's last letter written to our sister, Mimi, who lived in the outskirts of Vienna, the day they were ordered out of their apartment. Max wrote, "Mama und ich musten heute veg [Mama and I must leave today]." I never heard from them again. For many years I lived with the hope that they survived and lived in some remote country in Europe. I wrote some letters of inquiry, and in 1957, I was notified by an Austrian organization that there were records of their deportation to Riga in Latvia on December 3, 1941, but there were no records of return.

[Mom started to weep. We decided to end the interview and continue another day.]

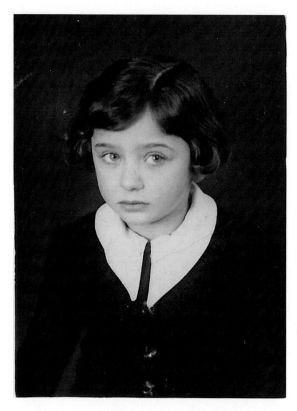

Ruthi Gerstl, my father's young cousin, lived with my parents for a few months in 1938 until their departure from Austria. She, her parents and four siblings were murdered by the Nazis in 1941. She was nine years old.

The Austrian passport, 1938, when Austria had become part of the Deutsches Reich [German Empire].

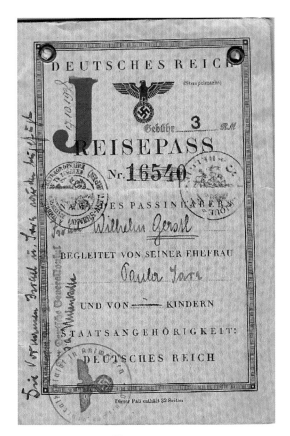

Names "Israel" and "Sara" were added
for further Jewish identification.

Copy of Mémé's [my paternal
grandmother] passport.

Vienna, November 9th 1938.

To the Secretary of

the Department of the Interior,

Canberra, Australia.

Respected Sir,

By the present I beg to apply to you with the
humble request to grant me kindly the permit to enter Australia
and for this purpose I beg to hand you enclosed my application
as well as my description of life, certificates of health ,
certificates of good conducts for me and my wife and copies of
testimonials.-

If I have the intention to establish myself in
Australia, I am able to base this intention on the fact, that
I shall be in a position to produce the necessary landing-money
and besides this I think that thanks to my abilities and capa-
cities I shall be in a position to earn my subsistence and will
not become a burden to the State in no way, the more as here
in Vienna I was one of the best cutter in Vienna, a fact which
I am able to prove on demand.-

I dare hope, that my petition will kindly be
considered and that the immigration into Australia will be
granted to me and my wife and thanking you in anticipation for
your goodness and hoping to receive your kind favourable reply
as early as possible,I am,

Respected Sir,

Yours most sincerely:

Enclosure: 1 application   Wilhelm G e r s t l
    "   2 certificates of health   Vienna, II. Heinstrasse 3 / 8
             2 "   of good behaviour   Germany.
             copies of certificates

Letter of application to immigrate to Australia.

54

. . .

The Geographic Journey - 1938 to 1947

CHAPTER IV

Crossing No Man's Land

JO: When and how did you finally leave Vienna?

Ma: We left middle December 1938. I took my backpack, and Papa took his briefcase, we locked up the apartment, and got on a train to our first stop, Köeln [*Cologne*], Germany.

JO: You were able to get train tickets? Weren't the Nazis at the train stations arresting Jews?

Ma: They could if they wanted to.

JO: How many hours on the train to Köeln?

Pop: Maybe six to eight hours. A beautiful city.

JO: Wasn't it really dangerous to go through Germany?

Pop: Yes, but we had to take that risk.

JO: Why did you go to Köeln?

Pop: Our guide arranged for us to stay there until all parties involved in the flight arrived. We were housed in private homes. The proprietors got paid, of course, but they were taking a huge risk. They could have gotten in big trouble for helping Jews.

JO: How long did you stay and how many in your group?

Pop: We stayed two weeks. There were about twenty people, eight or ten from Austria. On December 31, the guide came to pick us up. We traveled to Aachen, and had to go through a German checkpoint. We were ordered to undress and place all our belongings on a table. We had to show what we were taking into Belgium.

JO: I don't understand why the Germans allowed Jews to leave.

Pop: Immediately after the annexation of Austria and Germany, they hadn't implemented the 'Final Solution to the Jewish Problem' yet so they didn't care if Jews left, but they had no right to return. They also had to leave all their possessions in Austria for the Aryans. Eventually, the "Final Solution" was implemented and Jews no longer could leave; they were forced out by transports to the death camps where millions were killed.

JO: Did the guards at the checkpoint ask any questions about how you were planning to get into Belgium?

Pop: No. Our passport was in order. We had paid the guide a lot of money, and he had arranged everything. Who knows what arrangements he made. I had 300 schillings on me, and I placed the money on the table. The officer gave me 30 schillings, and he took the rest. He asked me if I wanted it sent to someone in Vienna, and I gave him my mother-in-law's address. She did receive it.

JO: Was Mom with you?

Pop: Sure.

JO: Were the men and women in the same room?

Pop: No, the women were separate.

JO: Did you have to take off all your clothes?

Pop: Not the underwear or trousers. They checked our pockets.

Ma: Tell her about the gold watch.

Pop: [*Laughing*] I didn't realize that I was standing in front of the officer with my gold chain-watch hanging out of my pocket. He said, "Do you have anything else to declare?" I was so nervous. I answered, "No, nothing." I checked inside my pockets to make sure, and they were empty. So he points to the dangling watch and says, "What's this?" I started to shake. I said, "I'm sorry, I forgot. I wouldn't stand here in front of you denying that I have anything if I knew that my watch was hanging out of my pocket." So he said, "I can see that you are nervous." He gave me my clothes back and let me keep the watch. We left the checkpoint and started our journey.

JO: Tell me about it.

Ma: It was nighttime when we reached the forest. It was patrolled by armed soldiers, and if you were seen, you risked getting shot. We walked silently in the darkness for ten hours through snow and ice, on treacherous, uneven terrain, fighting fallen branches and tree trunks, trenches and holes. The guide did his best to lead us as safely as possible through the area. Occasionally, we would see flashes of light that we assumed were coming from guards, and we would drop belly-down into the snow or crouch behind trees, and waited until they disappeared. One man in our group collapsed and died. We stopped and tried to help him, but there was absolutely nothing we could do to save him. He was very heavy and the rumor was that he had diabetes. Our lives were at stake, and we had no choice but to keep on going. We finally reached the border and took refuge in a barn, wet, cold and exhausted, waiting for the guide who had gone to get some taxis. When he returned, we bid farewell to each other, and parted ways. After a five-hour ride, we arrived in Antwerp.

•   •   •

Three Fugitive Families In Antwerp

Front row left to right: Paula Gutstein with daughter Ruthie Gutstein behind her; Grete Gerstl holding Cécile; my mother. Back row: Ernst Gerstl; David Gutstein; my father.

CHAPTER V

Antwerp 1939

JO: You arrived with a gold watch but no money. Did you have to sell it to get started?

Pop: Thankfully not. The Jewish Welfare Committee helped the refugees by paying their rent and giving them food. They placed us at a carpenter's house for a few days until we found a permanent home. It didn't take long before I found work and could pay for our living expenses.

Ma: Meanwhile, we would stand in line like beggars for meals. Rich people with diamonds on their fingers would serve us. We would get so much for lunch that we had enough for dinner as well.

Pop: I got a job with Mr. Mandelbaum, and he gave me lunch. Ma would bring home both our lunches from the committee, so we had plenty of food.

JO: Later on, did these rich people also have to flee Belgium?

Ma: Yes, they just had a little more time. A few days after our arrival, Papa and I met with the committee. We asked if we could live in the same house as Ernst and Grete. They had rented a room in a nice home that belonged to Mme Paula Van Stevens at 88 Marstaad, a suburb of Antwerp. She had another room for rent, and we took it. Grete was five months pregnant at the time.

Pop: I remember having to sleep three in one bed [*laughs*]. Why did we do that?

Ma: Our room wasn't available yet. Grete had gone to Ostend for a few days to visit her sister, Lisl, who lived there, and we had nowhere to sleep, so Ernie, you and I slept together in their bed [*laughs*].

JO: That must have been cozy! Tell me, how did you find your job with Mr. Mandelbaum?

Pop: The committee knew that I was a tailor, so they recommended me to him. He needed some suits for his two daughters. He was such a nice man. When the suits were finished, he asked how much he owed me. I didn't want payment because I was grateful that he was providing my meals at no charge. He told me that he had gone to the best tailor in Antwerp to find out the price of custom-made suits, and he knew that the cost was much more than his expenses for me. He said, "I am paying you, and I am not charging you for food." I also worked for his brother. By the time the Germans invaded Antwerp, we had saved some money. Ma took it with her to the camp in a pouch that I had made for her to wear under her clothes.

Ma: In the camp, I never took it off. I even slept with it.

Pop: I knew that the money might have to be hidden sometime in the future. We had to think ahead. We lived on that money.

JO: Did you work for anyone else?

Pop: Yes. Mostly Jewish people. There was an orchestra that ordered fifteen uniform jackets from me. I worked day and night and finished a jacket every two days. I kept very busy.

JO: Ma, how did you spend your time?

Ma: I would go to the Jewish Center with Grete almost every day. They offered interesting classes, including English, and there were concerts and plays. We would go to the park where we'd get together with friends. We felt welcome in Antwerp, and felt even more at home after my mother sent us our things. She mailed ten parcels filled with what we had left with her: clothing, hand-crocheted curtains that Rési had made for us, dishes, crystal, our sewing machine, and wedding gifts that we had not yet used. We lived as normally as possible under the circumstances, until Germany invaded Poland and we heard that they were approaching Belgium.

JO: When did Grete give birth?

Ma: She gave birth to Cécile on May 10, 1939.

JO: And you too became pregnant while you were in Belgium.

Ma: Yes. We had not planned to have a baby yet. Papa wanted stability. In Vienna, when things were good, he wanted to wait until he had saved the amount of money that he felt was necessary to provide his family with a proper home. He definitely did not want to start a family in Belgium with Europe at war. It was ironic that I became pregnant anyway, at the worst possible time. I honestly don't know how it happened [*Mom chuckles*]. We were happy about it, of course, but not long after we had gotten the news, we heard that the Germans were about to invade Belgium, and they would go after Jewish refugees. We knew that we would have to run away again, and I didn't know if I could do it in my condition. I had terrible morning sickness and was nauseous all the time. We had to make a terrible decision, but felt that it was the only solution. We decided to terminate my pregnancy. I went to a nurse who performed abortions. When I got there, she wasn't home. I felt that this was "beshert" [*meant to be*], a sign from a Divine Source not to carry out my plan. I made up my mind to go ahead with my pregnancy regardless of risks. I was going to carry my baby and die if that was my destiny. I turned around and went home.

JO: I'm sure glad you made that decision. How did Papa feel when he found out that you didn't go through with it, and why didn't he go with you?

Ma: He worried about it, but he accepted my decision. He couldn't go because he had to be at work, so Grete went with me. My bed was prepared when I got home, and water was simmering on the stove for my hygiene needs.

Pop: We almost ended up in Holland after that.

JO: How's that?

Pop: One day, at the Jewish Center, someone announced that a company in Rotterdam was looking for a cutter. I inquired about it and was granted an interview. Someone came from that company, watched me design and cut a pattern for a suit, and I had to get the suit ready for a fitting. They were very impressed with me, and I was offered the position. We accepted, thinking that Holland would be a safer place to live. We packed up and were ready to leave the following Monday.

• • •

Remnant of a boxcar used by the Nazis for human transport.

CHAPTER VI

Camp at St. Cyprien, Pyrénées-Orientales, France

JO: So you were ready to leave Antwerp and go to Rotterdam. Did you go?

Pop: No. The Friday before we were to leave, the Germans invaded Belgium and the border was closed. We were trapped and could no longer leave. Announcements were posted immediately ordering all Jewish men from Vienna and Germany to report to the police.

Ma: It was May 10, 1940, Cécile's birthday. She was one, and I remember buying her first pair of shoes — white shoes. I'll never forget that day. Papa and Ernie came home for lunch. The water had been shut off, so I was going to go to a nearby fountain and get some. Papa said, "Don't go. Ernie and I will get it." On the way, they planned to stop at the police station, as ordered. Grete and I prepared lunch and waited for their return, but they did not come back. We became extremely worried and asked our landlady if she knew what was going on. She said, "You don't need to cook. They aren't coming back. Didn't you hear that Austrian and German Jewish men are being deported?" We were shocked and did not believe it. News was always posted on kiosks in the streets, so Grete and I went to look, and saw the announcement ordering Jewish men to report to the armory immediately. It also said to bring food and clothing for 24 hours. We quickly returned home, and I packed the briefcase with some cans of sardines, chocolate, bread, a jacket, a little money and some toiletries. When Grete and I approached the armory, we saw so many women and children. The men were locked up in buildings. We knew that they were going to be deported, but we didn't know when or where. I happened to see a woman I knew from Vienna. She and her husband had a big fabric business there. She suggested that I give one of the Belgian guards 100 francs to find Papa and give him the briefcase. I had very little money on me, so she gave me what I needed.

On Sunday, when Grete and I arrived at the military building, hundreds of men were forcefully being marched to the train accompanied by armed Belgian soldiers. Women were throwing bundles of provisions, but the soldiers kicked the packages away. Those who tried to pick them up were struck with rifles. The men were pushed into the trains and crammed into boxcars. There were so many women and children crying, pushing and shoving, wanting to say good-bye, with men's hands reaching out the small windows trying to bid farewell.

Pop: We thought we were just going to check in at the police and then go home. When we arrived, they opened a door and said, "Go in there!" They pointed to a courtyard. We asked what was going on. They told us that we were not returning home. A few days later we were taken away.

JO: So you had no opportunity to see Ma again?

Pop: No.

Ma: We saw Papa and Ernst march with the rest of the men.

Pop: On the way, we were pushed and hit with revolvers if we didn't walk fast enough.

JO: Were they German soldiers?

Ma: They were Belgian Nazis. Posters had already been placed in windows of restaurants, cafés, and movie house that read "No entry to Jews and dogs." That's why we had planned to leave Belgium and go to Rotterdam.

JO: Did you have to wear the "Jude" yellow armbands?

Ma: No. They hadn't started that yet.

Pop: When we got to the train, we were pushed into cattle cars. There were no seats. We sat on the floor.

JO: Was it dirty?

Pop: What do you mean dirty? It was filthy from the animals. Besides, there were no toilets. You pissed and did everything in the wagon.

JO: How long did you travel?

Pop: About two weeks, with some stops.

JO: Did it stink?

Pop: So bad we could hardly breathe. There were sixty or seventy of us in there, no open windows, just cracks that let some air in.

JO: Did you get food and water?

Pop: Very little when we stopped, and that wasn't very often.

JO: Were you scared?

Pop: No. We were too busy trying to survive the hunger, the thirst, and lack of air.

JO: Did you know where you were going?

Pop: We knew we were being taken to a refugee camp in France. Along the way, we stopped in two camps – Villeneuve and Villemur – but they took us away from there. I remember arriving in the middle of the night at one of them. The land was part of a machine factory. At one time, machines were hidden in trenches, but when we got there, the trenches were empty. It was pitch black and we couldn't see a thing. While walking into the camp, many fell in and got hurt.

JO: Did you?

Pop: Yes. We were lucky that we did not break any bones.

JO: Was anyone injured on the train? Did anybody die?

Pop: Everybody in my wagon survived. We were so weak and sick that we could hardly stand up. The Germans had ordered the Belgians to paint "German Parachutists" on the outside walls of the train to give the impression that we were German prisoners of war. They knew that France hated the "Boches" — that was their derogatory name for the Germans — and labeling us "German parachutists" would insure that no one would help us poor souls trapped inside the train. We made a stop in Bordeaux. Through the cracks, we could see barrels of water covered with straw. We yelled and begged a French soldier on the platform to give us some. A few men shoved their arms through spaces between the slats offering him money. The soldier looked at us with scorn, kicked the barrel over, and we watched the water spill out.

JO: Couldn't he tell that you were not soldiers?

Pop: He only saw hands.

JO: Who was in your wagon?

Pop: All men, young and old, even little boys. Two weeks in and out of that stinken wagon until we arrived at St. Cyprien. Ernst was in a separate transport that arrived before mine because he was assigned to work in the kitchen. I knew I would end up with him eventually. They told us.

JO: What was the camp like?

Pop: Bad. It was in France near the Spanish border. There were hundreds of wooden barracks built on sand with no floors, no doors, just sand and hay to sleep on. Everything was surrounded by barbed wire. It was so big … big as a city … just barracks on sand by the water … so many barracks. It was so hot that everyone ran around naked.

When we arrived, we saw a pipe with just a trickle of water coming out of it. We were so thirsty that one would push the other out of the way if he took too long to drink. I don't know what kind of water it was but I didn't get sick from it. Many did. I saw Ernie and he said, "Go to Yod 22.* In that barrack, you will find my jacket on the floor, and underneath you will find some bread." I entered the barrack and saw that people slept on straw on the ground. Ernie had double straw because he helped carry it. I lifted his jacket and I saw six or seven loaves of bread, good white bread, wonderful bread. I ate a whole loaf, every little piece of it I was so hungry. Ernie returned from work at three. He had arrived at the camp one or two days before me, and had been put to work in the kitchen immediately. There were no dishes, so we ate out of tin boxes. There weren't enough for everyone, so three people ate out of one box. Little by little, more arrived, and eventually everybody got his own tin box

JO: Was the camp clean?

Pop: How could it be clean? There was sand everywhere, we had no toilets, just cans outside. There were insects in the barracks.

JO: How many men were in the camp?

Pop: Maybe two thousand, I don't know exactly.

JO: What kind of food did you get?

Pop: Soup. There was rice in it and beans, all kinds of stuff, and noodles. A good thick soup.

JO: No meat?

Pop: No meat.

JO: Did you get any breakfast?

Pop: A black coffee and a piece of bread.

JO: And lunch?

Pop: Soup.

JO: And dinner?

Pop: Soup again.

JO: You didn't get anything in between?

Pop: The soup was thick. I myself didn't need it because I got extra from Ernst. He told me to take my portion and give it to someone else. Next to my straw were two doctors, one on this side and one on that side. Ernie said, "I am done at three, and I will bring you soup, so give your soup one day to this one and one day to that one." At three o'clock, he would bring me a bottle of black coffee and soup. I had it good because Ernie worked in the kitchen. Besides that, Lisl would sometimes bring food for her husband, Fritz, and for us too.

JO: Who was Lisl and how could she bring food?

Pop: Grete's sister from Ostend in Belgium. Fritz was deported with me and Ernst, so she left Ostend and rented a room outside the camp. She would come visit with their son, Ben. It was allowed. Other women came to visit their men too. Don't forget, this camp was run by the French and they were not so strict.

JO: What did you do all day?

Pop: Nothing.

JO: Nothing? They didn't make you work?

Pop: No. Nothing.

JO: But Uncle Ernie worked.

Pop: He was in the kitchen.

JO: Didn't you do some cleaning?

Pop: I did nothing. All I did was straighten out my straw.

JO: So you sat around all day?

Pop: We sat around waiting, talking, we walked around. Sometimes we swam in the sea. It was the only way to wash. We had nothing to do...we were helpless and depressed.

JO: Did you have any idea why or what you were waiting for?

Pop: We would see trucks bringing transports of men and taking others away. We knew that those leaving were being taken to a camp not far away called Gurs. There was talk that from Gurs, the next stop was probably Auschwitz. It's funny, but most of us didn't care any more. We were tired of waiting...tired of not knowing...we wanted to get it over with.

JO: Were you afraid?

Pop: At first yes.

JO: Did you have any contact with Ma?

Pop: Not until June.

JO: What happened in June?

Pop: We were allowed to write and receive mail.

JO: How did you know where Ma was?

Pop: Through Uncle Henry and Tante Hilda in Nice.

JO: Please explain.

Ma: We were the last of the family to leave Vienna. Tante Rosa, Uncle Ludwig, Mémé, Uncle Henry and Tante Hilda had fled to France and when they got there, they wrote to us and sent us their addresses. In June 1940, when we were allowed to use the postal system, Papa and I wrote to them and told them where we were. They notified each of us and that's how we were able to correspond. Papa's letters gave me strength.

Pop: It was a huge relief for me to be able to keep in touch with Ma. Through me, she was able to let some of the women in her camp know that their husbands were in St. Cyprien.

JO: You once told me that there was a synagogue in the camp?

Pop: Yes, we set up a shul in a barrack. On Saturdays, it was our shul; on Sundays it was a church for the Christians. We shared the barrack. We didn't have a rabbi, just an Orthodox Jew who could lead the services. He had brought a Torah with him. Today it was a shul, tomorrow a church ... two religions together.

JO: Ma, what happened to you after Papa was deported from Belgium?

Ma: I knew that I had to get out of Belgium as soon as possible. There was no question in my mind that women and children would be next.

*Photo of Yod 22 page 97

Historical Information

Camp at St. Cyprien in Southern France

Source: Internet. *Jewish Traces, Mémoire et histoire des réfugiés juifs pendant la Shoah* [Memoirs and History of Jewish Refugees During the Shoah]

My father did not elaborate in his description of the camp. I wanted more details, so I did some research on the internet, and found the following information:

On May 10, 1940, Germany invaded Belgium. The Belgian police embarked on a massive wave of arrests of Jewish male refugees originating from Reich territories in Austria. An estimated 7,500 Jewish German/Austrian refugees, ages 16 to 65, were taken in this roundup, about 3,000 from Antwerp. The refugees were treated as spies or "suspect Germans." The journey by train in locked cattle boxcars from Antwerp to St. Cyprien took from 10 to18 days, depending on the convoy. This included stops at several transit camps. There were about 70 men per wagon; they suffered because of severe lack of water and food.

The St. Cyprien Camp was made up of thirteen sectors, separated from one another by barbed wire. Each sector consisted of 28 barracks, totaling 364. They measured 700 square feet to 1200 square feet. There were about 75 men per barrack, giving each man an average space of 2'x 6', just enough for a layer of straw. The camp had a theoretical capacity of 27,300.

A memorandum written on September 20, 1940, by former members of the Assistance Committees for Jewish Refugees from Brussels and Antwerp explained the deplorable sanitary conditions in the camp:

"Firstly, the geographical location at St. Cyprien camp could not have been worse. The sandy soil of a region subject to great climatic variation could never be suitable ground for a housing zone. The huts are made of planks of light wood with corrugated roofing and do not insulate against the wind, the frequent sandstorms and the cold. There is no floor, no bed, no mattress, not even straw mattresses. The internees sleep on a small layer of hay on the floor. There are no windows, lighting, heating, and these emergency shelters are true dens of microbes and infectious diseases carried by rats, bugs, lice and other vermin that also live in the camp. There is only one water tank for the whole camp, for which a bacteriological examination carried out in summer 1940 showed that the water was contaminated and therefore unusable. Nonetheless, this is the water that is used in the kitchen to prepare the food and to clean the cauldrons used for this purpose. The cauldrons are already rusty and the food contaminated with grime and grit because they have no lids. The walls, tables and work surfaces of the kitchen are made of wood that is damp and rotten, meaning that the kitchen is also infested with worms. The internees only have one container for food: only old tinned food cans.

The latrines are frequently only metal buckets without a lid placed between the huts, with the rare exception of a few wooden lavatories that are in no way more hygienic. The only disinfectant is the occasional use of potash chlorine. Epidemics arising from malnutrition and terrible hygiene are breaking out, and they affect a fifth to a quarter of the population. Stomach infections, loss of blood and considerable weakening of the internees are common, but this problem is classified as 'not dangerous' by the military authorities who register only 'some deaths'. During the summer of 1940, a serious epidemic of typhoid fever broke out and each day there were deaths, with the epidemic claiming hundreds of lives. At St. Louis Hospital in Perpignan alone, there were 40 deaths and 160 cases of illness. There were also cases of malaria, jaundice and trachoma."

Rabbi Kappel, a French military chaplain, in his memoirs, mentions the testimony of Rabbi Leo Ansbacher, interned in St. Cyprien with his brother, as follows:

"7,500 refugees chased from Belgium, accused of being spies, exhausted, arrived to the camp near Perpignan, met by locals screaming 'death to the German spies'. The living conditions in this camp situated on the shores of the Mediterranean were deplorable. The wooden barracks built on the sand were grouped into islets of 25 units, each islet separated by barbed wire. Sand penetrated everything, there was lack of water, typhus and dysentery emerged, the sick being evacuated to a hospital [St. Louis de Perpignan] worthy of the Middle Ages. There were 200 evacuees in the month of August. Mortality in the camp is elevated."

The following English translation was obtained from the internet: L'Association Philatélique de Rouen et Agglomération.

"It became extremely urgent to evacuate the internees, but one needed the serious [severe] floods which invaded the camp … from October 16 to precipitate the movement. The camp was closed on October 30th, 1940, and the internees were transferred to Gurs.

DISCOMFORT, PROMISCUITE, SALETE [filth], COLD…Such are the painful living conditions imposed on the internees in French camps! The majority supported [tolerated] it very badly: "the conditions under which one lives here are dreadful, it is the end of the culture," writes an internee of ST-CYPRIEN to Rabbi CHNEERSON on November 24, 1940.

Water badly filtered for drink and food; open W.C.; flies in quantity such as they are unbearable; mice, rats, chips and lice; insufficient, partially infested straw mattresses vermin; defective huts; malnutrition; miss [lack of] clothing and underclothing; almost complete absence of drugs, disinfecting and articles of hygiene.

Eighty five percent of the internees were reached [infected with] of dysentery in August 1940. At the same time, an epidemic of typhoid involved the hospitalization of 112 patients at the St. Louis Hospital of Perpignan. Seventeen died in less than three weeks. An antityphic [antityphoid] vaccination was practiced [administered] as from August 22 only.

Little time after, 150 internees were reached [infected] with malaria and lack of drugs did not make it possible to look after [treat] suitably.

A report of the doctors establishes that the water used in the camp was polluted by colon bacilli of fecal origin. The underground sheet [flow] of water was indeed in direct communication [contact] with stagnant liquid sheet [flow] of water located under the urinals and the latrines."

. . .

Château de Frémont

Quote from my mother: "Up on a hill stood a beautiful castle where the lieutenant and the guards lived. Any internee caught out of the stall after seven o'clock would be locked in the estate cellar for twenty-four hours."

Photo by my husband, Jerry Olson, taken on a pilgrimage with our daughter, Hilary, and her husband, Charles Mechler, and me, in 2008.

CHAPTER VII

Camp Frémont, Vallon-en-Sully, France

Ma: After the men were taken away, it was quiet as a morgue. No planes, nothing. I was devastated. I had to get out of Belgium and didn't know where to go or what to do. I heard on the radio that on Tuesday, May 14, a train was taking 1800 refugees to France. It was the last one going from Belgium. Our things were packed because we had gotten ready to move to Rotterdam, so I was ready to go. All I needed to do was find a way to get my luggage, as well as Grete's and her mother's, to the train station.

Some friends had a car and I asked if they would help us out, but there wasn't enough room for so much stuff. In the street, I saw a young man who had a cart. He agreed to take our things, and piled everything in. When we got to the station, we were told that there was no room for luggage, and we had to leave it behind. I was beside myself — we couldn't just abandon everything in the station! All the things my mother had sent from Vienna were in those boxes. I asked the young man if he would take it back to our landlady's apartment, and offered him the groceries that we had left in the cupboards as compensation — coffee, sugar, flour, etc. I hoped that someday we would be able to reclaim our possessions. He accepted the offer and I went back with him and gave him the groceries. I asked our landlady to store the luggage until further notice, and she agreed. I returned to the train and met Grete, her mother, and Cécile. We climbed into an open coal boxcar, no roof, no seats, no room to move, not knowing how long we would have to endure these hellish conditions towards an unknown destination. This was the start of our journey to Camp Frémont, Vallon-en-Sully, France.

JO: Why didn't you leave Belgium sooner?

Ma: We hoped that the Germans would not invade Belgium. Besides, we had no idea where to go. The Rotterdam opportunity came up, but too late. We didn't know it then, but it was a good thing; had we gone there, chances are we might not have survived the war.

JO: When you left on that train, what were you wearing?

Ma: The nights were still cold. I remember wearing a suit that Papa had made for me, and a coat. I was carrying my backpack with a little food in it, and a big red purse that Max had given me for my birthday.

JO: It seems like you were dressed up.

Ma: Women did not wear trousers then. Papa made my clothing, and everything was very elegant and well-tailored. I had packed a pair of Papa's warm socks and his wool hat in my big red purse.

JO: Where was the money you had saved while living in Belgium?

Ma: In the pouch that Papa made for me, attached to my garter belt. Our documents were hidden in there too. Papa always said, "You can lose anything, but not the documents." When he was deported, he had very little money on him.

JO: How long were you on that train?

Ma: Three days.

Pop: I was in the train much longer without any food.

Ma: We didn't have any food either and no bathrooms.

Pop: We did it in the train.

Ma: I didn't eat so I didn't have to go.

JO: What did people do if they needed a toilet?

Ma: We were constantly bombarded and there were air raids. The train would stop, everyone would jump out, run from the train and lie flat on the ground. Sometimes there was an opportunity to quickly take care of one's needs before getting back on. During travel, we had to do it in the wagon just like animals. People were screaming and crying. One woman went crazy. She urinated in a plate and ripped up her clothes. It was horrible. [*Mom pauses.*]

JO: Can you go on?

Ma: Yes. Three days in a dirty coal wagon, the sound of bombs nearby, no food or water, not knowing where we were going or if an explosion would kill us. We stopped in Paris for a few hours. It was night, and I remember screams … you couldn't see anything, but you could hear screaming. We saw houses burning. The only blessing was that the day I got into that train, my morning sickness stopped. I had been so sick until then. God helped me. I think it was May 17 when we arrived at Camp Frémont.

JO: Who gave the order to locate you there?

Ma: It came from Vichy, headquarters of the French government in the Free Zone under Philippe Pétain. The Germans had occupied Paris and the north of France.

JO: What was Camp Frémont?

Ma: It started out as a French refugee camp. By the time I left, it had become a detention camp.

JO: What was the difference?

Ma: A refugee camp held people until they were cleared of suspicious activity against France, and then they were free to leave. In detention camps, people would not be liberated and were held prisoners until eventual transfer to the death camps – there were about forty detention camps in France. Most refugees were liberated from Frémont fairly quickly, but not the Austrian and German Jews. There were orders that they remain because the Germans had convinced Marshal Pétain that Jews were enemies of France. As a result, Frémont became a detention camp for the sixty remaining Austrian and German Jews who were held until deportation to Camp Gurs.

JO: Tell me about your arrival at Camp Frémont?

Ma: The train stopped at a small railway station in Vallon-en-Sully. From there, we were taken to the Château de Frémont, a large estate past the village. This property must have belonged to wealthy people, but the owners were gone. Up on a hill stood a beautiful castle where the lieutenant and the guards lived. A little distance away, surrounded by barbed wire, was a large L-shaped building. It was a stable consisting of many stalls. There were a couple of barns on the premises as well. The weather was beautiful but cool. The countryside was lovely with fields and trees and a small forest. People over sixty, children, and pregnant women were placed in the stalls, six or seven women in a space big enough for one horse, and the rest of the people, maybe fifty to a building, were lodged in the barns, men and women separate. Grete, her mother, Cécile and I were together in one stall. I was in my fourth month. We slept on the floor — a cold cement floor covered with straw. My spot was near the sewer drain … no pillows, no blankets … [*To Pop: If I'm making you nervous, go on out!*] [*Pop leaves the room.*] It was so cold at night! All I had was my coat, Papa's hat and socks. Eventually, some Czechoslovakian carpenters were ordered to cut up logs for people to sit on, and when I got fat, they put some boards together and made me a sort of bed because I could not get up from the floor.

We got one glass of water a day to wash. Cécile was one year old, and Grete would bathe her in a dish. There were no toilets or outhouses, so the men were ordered to dig trenches and cut down branches to provide people with some privacy. You could see each other anyway, and I just couldn't go.

JO: So what did you do?

Ma: We were given an empty jam can to use in our stalls. Eventually, the carpenters built a couple of out-houses for daytime use. We had a seven o'clock curfew in the evening, until seven in the morning, so if we had to go at night, we had to relieve ourselves using the can. Any internee caught outside after seven would be locked up in the estate cellar for twenty-four hours. You can imagine how it stunk in a stall occupied by so many people, and no air circulation in the summer months when it was so hot.

JO: Were you given enough food?

Ma: I would get three glasses of milk per day because I was pregnant, and I think three slices of bread. By the time the milk came, there were huge flies in it. I couldn't drink it, and so I would give it to a woman who wanted it. She would fish the flies out and drink the milk. We got a little meat for lunch and some rice. There were always flies on the food. Because of my pregnancy, I also got three glasses of wine a day, but I didn't drink it because I thought it would harm my baby. At the beginning, I was thin and you couldn't tell that I was pregnant. People were saying that I must be having an affair with the lieutenant because I was getting special food. Of course, that wasn't true. I didn't eat much but eventually my stomach got so big, people thought I was going to have twins. There were a few Orthodox families who did not touch the food. After a while, the children looked like skeletons. I wasn't very hungry so I would give them some of my bread.

JO: Were you scared?

Ma: Yes, and I was sad. I didn't sleep much and I would cry at night. I can't describe what I went through emotionally … pregnant, no proper nourishment, imprisoned in a horse stall, sleeping on straw like the Virgin Mary, no washing or bathing, and worst of all, not knowing what was going to happen. Would I survive, would we get hit by a bomb, would I ever see Papa again, was I destined to give birth? Five months of this.

JO: Did the Nazis ever come to Frémont?

Ma: Yes. The camp had to be cleaned thoroughly before they came. Each stable had to be perfect. They would ask, "Who wants to go back to Belgium?" They would tell us that things were much better there. Meanwhile, the people who went back were eventually captured and sent to the gas chambers.

JO: Why did they inspect the camp if they had no control in that part of France?

Ma: They had indirect control. Germany took over Paris in June 1940, and the French surrendered. I don't know why, but the Germans agreed to take the north of France with Paris as their headquarters, and they would not occupy the southern portion. It was turned over to an anti-Semitic government headed by Marshal Philippe Pétain who was given administrative authority as long as it did not interfere with German rule. The city of Vichy was chosen as the capital of the "Free Zone." Pétain collaborated with the Nazis, and had no problem deporting Jews. In Paris, the French police cooperated with the Nazis, and thousands of Jewish French citizens were deported to the death camps.

JO: So Vallon-en-Sully was in the Free Zone region. How were the internees treated?

Ma: The lieutenant in charge of the camp was evil. The men were beaten and had to work very hard and long hours with very little nourishment. I remember an attorney and his mother. He had to scrub floors and if it didn't pass inspection, the lieutenant would beat him. This attorney was a big strong guy when we arrived, but he became so thin. I felt so sorry for him. Eventually, the lieutenant was replaced by a younger one who was much kinder and eased up on some rules. For one thing, we were allowed to use the outhouse at night. Six weeks after he took over, he gave another pregnant woman and me permission to walk into the woods accompanied by a soldier so that we could pick berries. We would make a fire over two stones with a little wood and cook them. They were so sweet and good. We were also given better food.

After a couple of months, some guards went to town to buy lemons and tomatoes for us. I gave one some money to buy material and supplies so that I could make myself a maternity dress. I had outgrown my suit, and had nothing to wear. The Czechoslovakian refugees were gentiles and didn't like the Jews. I was lucky though. They liked me because I spoke a little Czech and I always laughed even though my heart was heavy. They thought I had a great sense of humor. In preparation for your birth, they made me a crib out of wood and branches. Before they were liberated, they burnt what they had built for their own comfort so that the remaining Jews would not get them, but they gave me a couple of things.

JO: You once told me that your pregnancy saved your life. How did that happen?

Ma: I told you that little by little everyone but German and Austrian Jews were liberated from camp Frémont. Included were pregnant women, but they had to be examined by a military doctor for confirmation that they were indeed pregnant. There were five expectant women, three of which left early on. I knew that I eventually would be liberated too, but months went by and the doctor did not come. I dreaded the possibility of having to give birth in the camp. There was a medical student who was ready to help me through the delivery, but all he had available were some rusty instruments. I was sure that if I went into labor under these conditions, you and I would die. When Grete, her mother and Cécile were released, I was happy for them, but I was devastated because I couldn't leave. I was so upset that I fainted. Eventually, more people I knew left, and I remained alone, sure that I would never get out.

JO: Why were Grete, her mother and Cécile released and you were not?

Ma: I don't know. Maybe because Cécile was born in Belgium.

JO: Continue.

Ma: When just about everyone had left, the other pregnant woman and I were moved into a barn occupied by men and women. There was no privacy. The toilets were about a half a mile away, and I would walk there in the middle of the night because I was too embarrassed to use a can in front of other people.

In September, Papa, who had escaped from St. Cyprien and was in Nice, wrote a letter to the lieutenant pleading that I be allowed to leave. I think that letter might have helped because a week later, a doctor came to examine me. He signed a document stating that conditions at Camp Frémont were intolerable for a pregnant woman. He told me that I might deliver at any hour and it would be wiser if I stayed in the camp. I said no way; that would be the end of my baby and me. I couldn't wait to get out of there, no matter what would happen — anything but give birth in the camp. The lieutenant signed a release and gave me a Sauf-Conduit [Safe Transit]. This happened about three weeks before I gave birth to you. I immediately notified Papa to pick me up.

JO: How did you notify him?

Ma: By telegram. Hilda came from Nice by train. Papa couldn't come because he couldn't risk getting caught — he was a runaway from St. Cyprien on the loose. Hilda lived in France legally, so she was allowed to travel. She arrived, was given a meal, and we left Camp Frémont in Vallon-en-Sully on September 26, 1940.

Shortly after my liberation, the sixty people remaining in the camp were transferred to Camp Gurs. I have two letters from camp colleagues confirming this. They were written to congratulate me on giving birth to my new baby. Such fine people and wonderful letters. I think Papa was jealous because he didn't want me to answer them. Even today I regret not writing back.

JO: How do you know what happened to them?

Ma: My friend, Dr. Henri Korn, wrote that "the people that I left behind", including himself, were no longer in Vallon-en-Sully, but had been transported to Gurs. Had I not been pregnant, there would have been sixty-one from Camp Frémont.

The old train station where the refugees from Belgium arrived in Vallon-en-Sully, May 1940. The rails and building are no longer in use. A new building stands nearby, and new rails run parallel to the old ones.

Abandoned stables at the estate of Frémont on our visit in 2008. Hilary, Chip, and I standing in the distance. *Photo by my husband Jerry Olson 2008.*

Stables at the estate of Frémont in Vallon-en-Sully circa 1960. We showed my mother this photograph when we found it on the internet in 2005, one year before her death at the age of 96. She identified her stall as the one in the corner on the right.

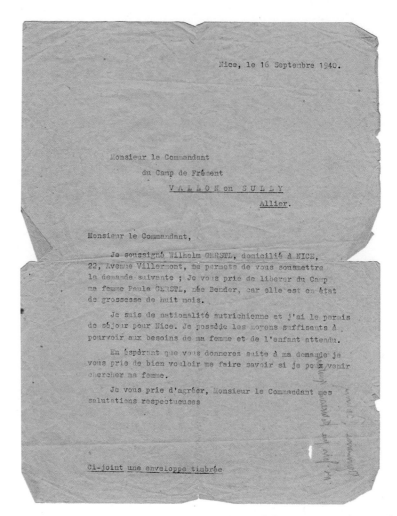

A carbon copy of the letter to the Commandant of the camp sent by my father.

Nice, September 16, 1940

To the Commandant of Camp Frémont
Vallon en Sully
Allier

Dear Sir,

I, the undersigned, Wilhelm Gerstl, living in Nice, 22 Avenue Villermont, do respectfully request that you liberate my wife, Paula Gerstl née Bender, from the camp, as she is in her eighth month of pregnancy.

My nationality is Austrian, and I have a permit to stay in Nice. I do have sufficient means to take care of the needs of my wife and forthcoming child.

I am hoping that you will agree to my request, and I would appreciate if you would let me know if I can come to pick up my wife.

Please accept, Mr. Commandant, my respectful salutations.

Enclosed a stamped envelope

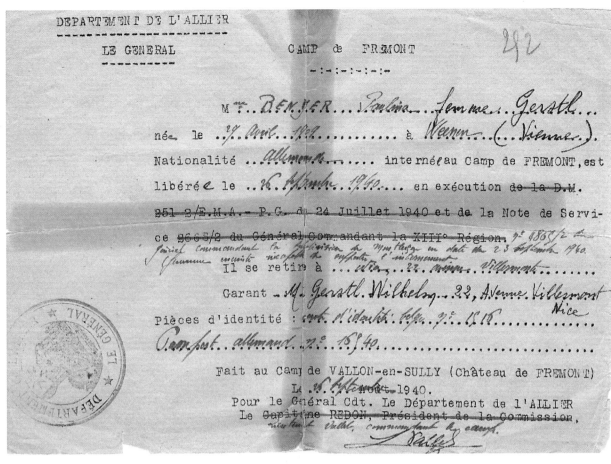

This document, issued ten days after my father's letter to the commandant, liberated my mother. It was issued upon a doctor's confirmation that she was pregnant. She was in her eighth month.

CAMP DE FRÉMONT

Mrs. Bender Pauline female Gerstl,

Born April 29, 1909, in Vienna

Nationality German interned at Camp de Frémont, is liberated the 26th of September, 1940, pursuant to the Note of Service # 486512 of the General Commandant of Montlucon, the 23rd of September 1940. Pregnant woman unable to withstand internment.

Her destination is Nice, 22 Avenue Villermont

Guarantor: Mr. Gerstl Wilhelm, 22 Avenue Villermont, Nice

Identification: Belgian identification card #1516

German passport #16540

Document executed at Camp Vallon-en-Sully (Château de Frémont)

September 26, 1940

For the General Commandant. Department of ALLIER

Lieutenant Vallel, Commandant of the camp
L. Vallel

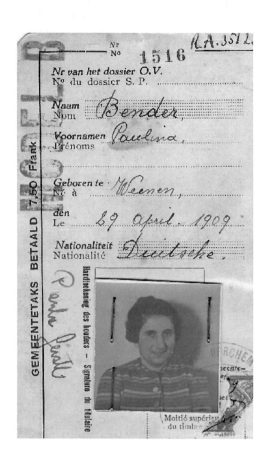

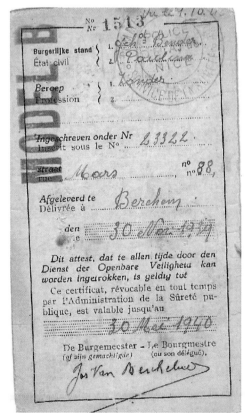

Identification cards were issued to foreigners in Belgium. There is an insertion [*shown below right*] on my mother's, added by the Prefect of Police in Vallon-en-Sully on May 28, 1940, stating that she is excluded from internment due to her pregnancy, but needs examination and confirmation by a French doctor.

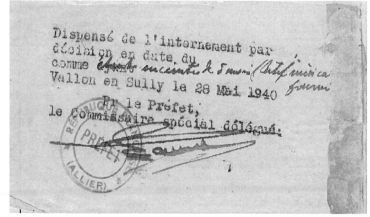

Temporary Safe Transit issued to Mom upon her liberation

French Republic
TEMPORARY SAFE-TRANSIT
Police Department Vallon-en-Sully

Valid for travel September 26, 1940 til October 2, 1940

To go from Vallon-en-Sully to Nice.

Name and Surname: Bender, Pauline

Nationality: German

Address [in Nice]: 22 Avenue Villermont

Profession: None

Method of Travel: Train

The commander of the police brigade

. . .

Historical Information

Camp at Gurs, Basses-Pyrénées

Source: Internet. *L'Association Philatélique de Rouen et Agglomération*

Built in one month and a half on a ground of almost 80 hectares and placed under the direction of Commander Davergne, this vast camp will be operational as of April 1939 with the arrival of 980 Spanish internees.

April 16, GURS gathers already 4,659 refugees and there are more than 15,000 on April 25. The forecasted manpower of 18,000 people will quickly be exceeded to reach 18,985 men on May 10, 1939.

Four-hundred and twenty eight huts had been built to accommodate them, including 46 reserved for the troops. A 1,700 m long road was created, and a 3 kilometers railway posed. Two hundred and fifty kilometers of barbed wire surrounded the camp.

If the living conditions appreciably improved compared to ARGELES and ST-CYPRIEN, they do not remain less precarious about it: no lighting in the huts, severely rationed water. The internees not being able to make a suitable toilet must fight permanently against the lice, the bugs….and the rats!

An insufficient and badly balanced food added to the lack of hygiene causes diseases and generates a significant number of neuroses and obsessional behaviors.

After having lodged Spanish refugees, the CAMP OF GURS is used by the regime of Vichy to intern political prisoners and Jews. It is the most important camp of the south of France.

As of October 1940, nearly 6,500 expelled German Jews of the country of Bade, Palatinat, and the Saar, arrive, within the framework of Operation Burckel. They will be followed, December 19, 1940, by the Spanish internees of ST-CYPRIEN after closing of this camp for medical reasons.

In his survey of the Jewish camps in July 1942, DANNECKER will declare: (Note: Dannecker is identified in WIKIPEDIA as Theodor Dannecker. He was an SS Hauptsturmführer [captain] and one of Adolf Eichmann's associates who became one of the most ruthless and experienced experts on the "Jewish Question," and his involvement in the genocide of European Jewry was one of his primary responsibilities.)

"The huts are in very bad condition. According to the direction of the camp, the absorption capacity of the camp is consequently strongly reduced. Total number of internees [Jewish]: 2,599 including 1,912 German subjects, and 335 other deportable. It should be noticed that of 1,912 Jews of ex-German nationality who almost all come from Palatinat, are more than 55 years old." From August 1942 to March 1943, six convoys will transport 3,907 Jews, men and women, towards Auschwitz via Drancy. November 1943, the camp is dissolved and the internees are transferred to Camp of Nexon. It preserves, nevertheless, until the Release, 229 gypsies, political prisoners and "common right." During the winter 1940-1941, 800 Jews died in GURS.

Over 1,000 Jews are buried in the cemetery at Gurs.

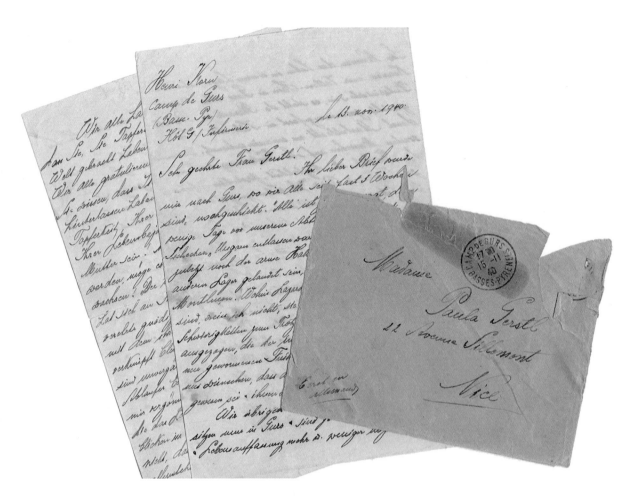

Letter sent to my mother in Nice by Dr. Henri Korn,
a Camp Frémont colleague transferred to Gurs.

Camp de Gurs
(Basse-Pyn)
Hol G/Infirmerie

November 13, 1940

Very honored Mrs. Gerstl,

Your kind letter was forwarded to me at Gurs where we all arrived nearly three weeks ago. "All" is an exaggeration, because a few days prior to our deportation, the Czechs and Hungarians were released, among them H. Gross, and at last the poor Hall. Gross supposedly ended up in another camp, Hall in a hospital in Montluçon. I do not know where Lagarowitsch and the remaining people went. In spite of all difficulties, they moved out some time ago with the enthusiasm that hope brings, as the previously interned breathed in their newly won freedom. Let us wish that fate was kind to you and will continue to be kind.

We, the remaining from Germany and Austria, are now in Gurs and, depending on one's temperament and philosophy of life, are more or less unhappy. You know the life in a camp, but you know only Vallon. Here in Gurs, there are supposedly 14,000 internees, there are barracks and barracks in rows combined into islets. The islets are separated from each other by barbed wire. Inside people are waiting for their release, hoping for freedom, for the possibility to be able to work productively, to build their life in dignity. The wheels of life roll on, time passes, the older ones perceive with great sorrow that the length of time for the creation of a worthwile life is getting shorter. Therefore, there develops the "camp sickness" that occurs because the hard, pitiless reality is replaced by unproductive discussions, by creating rumors, and above all, by letting the desire for freedom become the reason to dream and believe that which, unfortunately, can never become reality. It is hard, very hard to have to live that way. It is even harder to endure due to painful disappointments, due to the defeat of France. The picture of our future has become darker.

We were all especially pleased that you, the brave one, was able to deliver your little girl normally and that she is well. We all congratulate you with all our heart. You know that you left in Frémont only friends, only admirers of your courage, of your liveliness, your female kindness, and of your acceptance of life. May the little one be like her mother and remain healthy and happy, and may she grow towards a better future. The deepest purpose of the life of a woman realized itself in you. Let me wish you, admired gracious lady, that the life of your child stays tied to the thread of happiness. True human values are everlasting and may the ups and downs of historical periods not affect you. I do not know whether it will be granted to me to climb over the wall of bitter suffering which life has imposed upon us, and reach over into a future better world, but I have no doubt that the better world will be opened in the future to your child. Therefore, don't let the happiness of motherhood be influenced negatively by the Now, but be proud that you have been able to fulfill your destiny in the Now!

After a long time, I have received news again from my wife. Let me thank you from my heart for your good care. I thank only you that the time without news from her was at least cut short. You should know that, here in Gurs, are a few thousand Jews. Jewish women up to the age of 99 years expelled from German territory arrived with us. A new worry for all of us is if this new wave of terror will also reach Vienna. I have to back up. Mme Schoneman is here in camp. Mme Nasscu, accompanied by her husband, was released a few days before us. It is unknown to me how she is doing.

Once again, the heartiest thanks and again congratulations from all the camp comrades. I remain with best regards to your husband.

Sincerely yours,

H. Korn

Letter of congratulations sent to my mother from a Camp Frémont colleague in Gurs.

Gurs November 14, 1940

Dear Mrs. Gerstl,

I was so happy to hear that you have become a happy mother. I can imagine the happiness that you, your husband and entire family must feel. Be happy that this circumstance freed you from the camp. Meanwhile we were transferred. The difference is huge but what can we do. I am sending you and your husband my heartfelt Mazel Tov. May the child bring you all the happiness and may you only have Simchas. That is not only my wish, but the wish of the entire Camp Frémont where everyone loved you. Stay well and I send you my best regards.

(Signature cut off)

LETTERS

WILLY AND PAULA GERSTL

CAMP ST. CYPRIEN/NICE/CAMP FRÉMONT, JUNE 1940 TO SEPTEMBER 1940

Mail sent within France was allowed, including to and from detention camps in the Vichy governed region. My Aunt Hilda and Uncle Henry, who had left Vienna before my parents, wrote to them after settling in Nice, and sent their address. When my parents arrived at their respective detention camps, they wrote to Hilda and Henry to let them know where they were. Through cross correspondence, my mother and father learned of each other's whereabouts.

My mother saved most, if not all, of my father's letters sent to her in Camp Frémont, and he managed to save two of hers. He did not remember what happened to the rest.

The reader will notice that, at times, Ernst addresses his wife as Sali. That was her given name. For reasons unknown to my cousin Cécile, her mother preferred the name "Grete."

This photo was taken after the war in 1947. These were family members who were in Nice in 1939.

Front row far left is my uncle Ernst Gerstl, without his wife, Grete, who lost her life in 1942. Seated in the middle is my aunt, Rosa Holzer, and her husband, Ludwig, is standing in the back row far left. Standing behind Rosa is my cousin Cécile Gerstl, who was 1 ½ at the time, and behind her, my uncle and aunt, Henry and Hilda Gerstl. My father's sister, Laura, seated front row far right, had fled to Palestine and was not in France in 1939.

Mémé, my paternal grandmother.

July 10, 1940

My dear Paula and Sali,

We have just written a card but I'm so worried because we have not received any letters from you. The only consolation is that this is happening to everybody here. Naturally, dear Paula, I am doubly worried about you. At least, is there somebody there that helps you and do you have enough to eat? Can you buy anything? Do you have any money? I could suffer through anything if only I had news from you. What's new with you, dear Gretel, and the child and your mother? In one of your letters, dear Paula, you write that you can laugh again. Is it true? I read your letter daily about our things. Don't worry. First of all nothing is lost yet, and secondly I will provide for you again. Do you have mail from your mother, Rési and so forth? I don't want to bother you with more questions, so I will tell you a little about us. We have been in this third camp for six weeks. We are doing well. Gluckselig, Bergel's son-in-law who traveled with us, is in my barrack. He works in the kitchen and that's why we are doing well. There is no work here but today Ernst and I have food fetching duty. For that we get a double portion. We can bathe as much as we want in the sea, but I don't take advantage of it because of my stomach. We get red wine everyday. There are seventy people in our barrack and I am used to it by now. I don't argue with anybody. I know a lot of people here, for example, May, Loewe, the two Jauls, Ricsi Riegler, Hirschl, Herschendorfer, Blatt and Landau. I received a card from my mother from Oberon. She tells me that they will probably return to Nice. If only we were at that point! I would advise you, when you too will have the possibility, to contact Nice. Maybe the proper authorities could give you a Right for Asylum and then you could travel there. I wish that with all my soul.

How is your health? I am sure that we will be happy as can be soon, and that we will be able to retrieve all of our belongings from Belgium. Please write me in detail and be extremely careful with our documents. I am a little uneasy because, except for my Belgian identification card, I have no other papers. I have not received my Vienna citizenship certificate yet. Ernie, on the other hand, has everything. If possible, send me an authorized document, but only if you have the opportunity, and use registered mail — no other way. Also, send me a stamp for abroad so that I can write your mother. Should you be free and have some money, send me some cigarettes. I have little money and need to save. However, I don't want you to sacrifice anything, as it isn't that important. It won't be that long and we will be together. How happy I would be to go for a walk with you, also during the day[*my father jokingly had told my mother that when she gets round as a barrel he would only go for a walk with her at night*]. Ernst went picking peaches, and I have to leave some room for him in this letter.

Thousands of kisses,

Willi

Note from Ernie

Dear Sali, Paula and mother,

I just returned from picking peaches. We get six pieces per man. Because Gluckselig gets double, it is better for us because we share everything. I too was a cook in the first two camps, and in one or two days I will be doing that again here. How is the dear child? Hopefully that poor child has what she needs. If you have money, don't sacrifice anything and buy what you need. Don't worry about me.

That's all for now,

Ernie

• • •

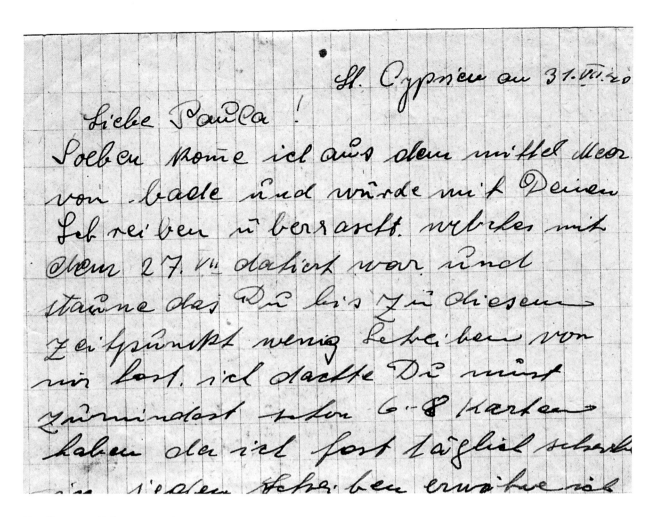

St. Cyprien July 31, 1940

Dear Paula!

I just came out from bathing in the sea and your letter of July 27 was a surprise. I can't believe that you have received so few letters from me. You should have gotten six to eight cards, as I write to you almost daily. In every letter, I mention that I have enough money because I got some back. Rosa sent us a Permission of Stay, and our documents are at the tribunal for inspection. I gave Henry's name as a recommendation, and I have to wait now. I am writing in a hurry because Lisl is taking the letter with her. How are you? I am waiting for the answers to the questions that I asked in the previous letters.

Many kisses,

Your Willi

Dear Gretel,

I hope you are right about us having a boy. God should help us that we will be together again , and then I will tease you. We hope to be liberated in four weeks, if not earlier (meanwhile he escaped).

Many kisses,
Your Willi

Many kisses to little Cécile and your mother.

Note from Fritz

Dear Grete,

Imagine how happy I am that I have my beloved wife and son close by. Unfortunatly, I am not free yet. Lisl is working towards freedom for the three of us. Hopefully she will be successful with some results soon. We still don't know anything about Lilly and Paul [Fritz's sister]. Stay well, also your mother, and eat well. Looking forward to a reunion soon.

Kisses to all,

Fritz

Addition from Willi to Paula

Too bad that the two letters did not arrive. You can't imagine how happy I am with your letters as I am curious about everything and stay up all night thinking. We will be happy yet. Have you heard from your mother and Max? Tomorrow I will write again. I kiss you.   Willi

Note from Ernst

My dear Sali,

I just received your card and am hurrying to answer it. I am happy that the commissary is open again, and that you can buy something for yourself and for the child. Dear Sali, you complain that I write so little and Willi writes more. You know that I never wrote much. You ask if I feel better. You would not recognize me. I look so well, and I got fat from working in the kitchen. Did the child suffer much with her little teeth, and does she have curls? I can't understand why you receive so little mail from me. I write every day. Why does your mother look so bad? Don't you get lung hash there? Dear Sali, I often ask you if you have clothing and shoes for the child, and if you were able to take her new coat with you? Yesterday, we received cigarettes from dear Hilda, although that was not necessary because we get enough here and have enough money. We also got mail from Henry who tells us that he sent us 50 francs. My dear child, you ask if I still have the jewelry. Of course I do. I have everything because I got the money back. A lot of women with children come here to visit their men. They suffer a lot because they have to sit around on sand, and sleeping accommodations are very bad. If you can, go to Nice but absolutely don't come here. I hope when I'm freed to probably go to Nice. Today we took a picture and I hope I look good on it, because I am a handsome guy, right? I believe that you are happy with me. I kiss you and my beloved child.

Regards to Paula. I hope she is well. Regards to mother.

Your Ernest

INTERNEES OF "YOD 22"

This photo was probably taken shortly after the men's arrival to St. Cyprien in May 1940, as they still seem in fairly good shape. Uncle Ernst is standings in row three, fifth man from the left, wearing a hat. Yod is a Hebrew letter used as a symbol for "Jew". Photos were taken for propaganda purposes to show how well the inmates were treated.

St. Cyprien August 2, 1940

Dearest Paula,

I have a feeling that I will be getting a letter from you this afternoon. I dreamed of you all night, and I got up a little earlier to get my morning routine over with. You will laugh but it really takes me a long time because there is no one here to serve me! First of all, straighten the straw, shake the cover, go to the water pump, then breakfast. Today it wasn't so bad because Lisl brought me a yellow biscuit from town. By now it's 9 o'clock. Soon we can go to the sea. Naturally I can't take advantage of it every day because I easily catch cold and my stomach gets upset. When I do go, it's mostly in the afternoons. I'm happy that I can swim now, and how proud I would be if you could watch me. I can't imagine that you can't go swimming. It is so hot. Do you ever have the opportunity? I have already bought a toothbrush. I'm telling you this because I think you are probably worried that I'm letting myself go. I can assure you that we are keeping clean even in this desert. Ernie and I made an inquiry on Sunday morning to find out if we can get out because Henry served in the military and we have family in Nice. Our papers were returned with no decision and we were told we still have to wait. I had already imagined all kinds of things, for example a good goulash and dumplings, egg gnocchi and salad, and coffee with milk. You will certainly now say that the way to a man's heart is through his stomach, but, to be honest, I would eat dry bread to be near you.

Mr. Loewe was here and told me that his wife is in Antwerp; also Mrs. Klemens. Last week, people who wanted to go back to Germany registered. About four hundred men went back. Today there is another registry. Because we are both in France, I am not considering it; we will get together easier and faster if we stay where we are. I am not envious of those who returned to Antwerp.* Mr. Loebl, whom I left in the second camp, wrote me and asked if I know where his wife and child are. I think that because so many women remained in Antwerp, they are probably still there, and I told him so. Many people are slowly being let out of here, but mostly Poles and different nationalities – we will also have our turn. Regarding time off, we get one day, but I don't use it because it is not worth going into town for a few hours and spend money. I'd rather save for the return trip to Nice. I was happy to hear that the concession in your camp is open again. I beg you not to spare anything for yourself!

Mrs. Steffi and Mrs. Nussbaum are still hanging around here and can't free their husbands. I also feel sorry for Lisl. Ben is very smart and brings us soda pop. He sometimes sleeps with Fritz in the barracks. We heard that women in Gurs are slowly being liberated. Hopefully that will happen in your camp as well soon. I am already restless because time is passing and you are still there. I would be happy if you would already be with my mother in Nice. If I knew that Ludwig were back, I would write him to pick you up. That's why I'm anxious to get news from Nice and from you telling me in detail how you are and how you feel. I wrote you everything to let you know that we are in good shape. Meanwhile you must have received much mail from me.

I kiss you a thousand times and am awaiting our happy reunion. Your Willi

Dear Grete,

I see Lisl everyday. She is outside the camp. Don't worry, everything will work out; you must be patient. Ben is very good. How is Cécile? She must be adorable by now. I hope we get a partner for her [he wishes for a son]. God should give me the luck to be with my wife when she gives birth. I hope, by then, to be free. They can't feed us here forever. Everything else, your husband should write to you. Write how you are doing. Your mail system in your camp does not seem to be very good.

Best regards, your brother-in-law Willi

Dear Paula,

It is afternoon and your anxiously awaited letter arrived which you added to Mr. Wasserman's. I am certain that you barely receive one quarter of my mail. I believe you when you say that you are nervous, but you have to stay strong. You know what a bundle of nerves I am and I have to control myself. The liberation will come sooner than you think; it will happen overnight. I am worried because Grete is so nervous. She usually doesn't take everything so seriously. But patience – don't take everything so seriously either. In 24 hours, possibly one thousand men are voluntarily going back to Germany.*

Kisses, Willi

---

*Most of the inmates who left St. Cyprien and returned to Belgium and Germany were eventually rounded up by the Nazis and sent to the death camps.

St. Cyprien August 3, 1940

Dear Gosherl! [German term of endearment]

Today, Saturday, I got your letter at lunchtime, and I read it three times. It really cheered me up. Ernst is amazed that a half hour went by and I didn't sit down to write you back. He was especially astonished that you had soup, veal and rice for dinner. He wonders if you are not joking. I would be happy to believe that it is true. As I see it, you also have meager weeks. You have to make sure that you always have a reserve of food. I'm happy that you and the child [*Cécile*] get a glass of milk. See if you can get some canned milk. We have to look out for ourselves to keep our strength. You write me how happy you are with mail – I feel the same way. You must be getting a letter a day from me because I always write and think of you. I don't have to flatter you because you know how devoted I am to you, especially now. Be strong, we will soon be together. Tomorrow, Sunday, or Monday, a second transport of one thousand men who volunteered to return to Germany is leaving. [*Thank God Papa did not volunteer.*]

People are constantly advising each other here. For me, going back to Germany does not apply as you and I are both interned in France. Should you have this option, I leave the choice to you. [*Pop commented that had she wanted to leave Camp Frémont and go to Germany, he would have volunteered as well.*] Everything will be more understandable soon – it is better to wait a little longer. Otherwise, we are well and often are visited by Lisl who lives outside the camp. She brings us all kinds of foods that we haven't seen in months – for example, an egg, etc. We still look very good. This afternoon we even bought some cocoa, but it was not as good as I make it. But it didn't matter; I will make you some soon, for you, for my son [*he was sure they were having a boy*], and for me.

Grete writes me that you wear lipstick. You must send me a lip print as you used to. Why do you write that no one is thinking about you but me? First of all, I am sure everyone is thinking of you, and secondly I always think of you. I think I have always been good to you, but when we will be together, you won't recognize me any more. I will be even better. Whatever we missed, we will catch up.

Write me the truth about your situation, smile, and be happy. I'm interested to hear more about your camp. That's all for now. Have a happy day. See you soon.

Willi

Dear Gretel,

Thank you for writing a little more this time. We often used to fight, and I would love to be able to do that again. If I didn't go to see Lisl once in a while, I wouldn't even remember what a woman looks like. It's a good thing they give us BROM [*product to reduce sexual drive*]. I would also love to have the opportunity to have Cécile get on my nerves. You write that your mother has diarrhea. I have good advice for her – it's because of the climate. Everyone here wears a stomach binder. I wear one too, day and night, even in the biggest heat. It was one of your terry cloth towels. When possible, have her drink red wine. Write me soon. Best regards from me, your dear "Mr. Brother-in-law." Many kisses to Cécile. Willi

. . .

St. Cyprien August 9, 1940

Dear Paula,

I am writing ahead today, but I am not sending my letter until I get yours. Actually, it is very quiet in my barrack today because twenty of our colleagues have left us. There was a nice parting celebration that went on until two o'clock to a quarter to three. About 1300 men are going back to Brussels-Antwerp. They are mostly men whose relatives remained there. Among them from our barrack, Jaul, Lowe, Klemens, Flatov, and Reich. To tell you the truth, I envy these men who are probably going to be reunited with their wives. They all volunteered to go. Supposedly, there will be a second transport. Naturally, you and I must think ahead and take everything into consideration. Ernst and I will not volunteer before we know what will happen to you, Gretel, etc. I think it is better for us to stay. I feel that we will know more in one or two weeks. I wrote you a card today as well, asking you to send me a certificate, but not an official one because I don't want it found out that one day we might disappear from here. The rules are different every day, and I am positive that you too will be freed one day, and very soon. I actually cried during the farewell speeches. I could not even properly say good-bye to my bunkmate, but today I went swimming and I feel better.

Just now, the young Wasserman came to see me. He makes cocoa and I am his steady customer. Today, two letters arrived at the same time — one from July 31st, and one from August 2nd. I thank you for answering my questions, but I am very angry with you. Why did you not tell me sooner that you do not have a blanket? Unfortunately, there are no visitation hours for women today because a commissioner is supposed to come, but tomorrow, I will ask Lisl to see if she can get a blanket for you in town. Also, why did you not write to Nice? Ludwig has some blankets. It is getting cold at night. Do you at least have a bale of straw? You write that it must be fun here. You know my nature. I worry all the time and I feel so bad that you have the brunt of the burden. Don't despair; we have to hope for luck. Do you have an infirmary? A second transport is scheduled, but we have no news from the first one. Ernst asked Lisl to send a package. We get grapes now, a nice beet for 175 francs, one egg for 2 francs. I have too many tomatoes, as I do not eat them, so Ernie has more. We have to get strong. Things are not as expensive here as by you. Write me immediately if you need money. I can tell by your handwriting how nervous you are, and I sit here and can't do anything about it. Don't be upset thinking that I will only be your Gerstl until the little one comes. For me, you are my little Gerstl just as before, and, on the contrary, you will be even more after. If there will be no other alternative, we will also register to go back to Belgium, but meanwhile, we will wait a little longer. You ask where Mrs. Lobl is. She is in Antwerp. Mr. Lobl wrote to me asking if I know where his wife is. I hope you are happy with my letter. Now I am going to have breakfast — cocoa and one egg. Please write me immediately or to Ludwig about the blanket, and buy yourself something to eat. Meanwhile, I send you many kisses, Your Gerstl.

Best regards to Grete and kisses to Cécile.

. . .

Nice, August 29, 1940

Dear Paula,

Yesterday, I wrote you immediately after my arrival, and hope that you have received my letter. I started working at Henry's today, and already have a different picture of the situation. I am glad that you are not here yet, although my heart aches. First of all, it is very difficult to get permission to stay in Nice, and I have no idea how this will happen. Secondly, I can't ask Ludwig, even though he has been very good to me, to stay with him and Rosa. Gretel and Ernst live in Mama's room [Mémé]. I sleep with Mama in the dining room. The apartment is very nice. I'm looking for a room, and if we can stay in Nice, I will do everything to prepare for your arrival so that you won't have any worries when you get here. It will be best if you wait for further news from me. I wrote you about the money. I'll leave it up to you. If you know a dependable person, maybe he or she can deliver it to me so that I can register at the police. If you can't send it, don't worry. I'll owe money a little longer. I hope to get more work and start saving soon. Nice is a fantastically beautiful city, but everything is difficult. Gretel told me that you are well, so please don't be impatient and wait a little longer. I must stop writing now, as it is almost the sabbath.

I kiss you a thousand times,

Your, Willi

I will write you again tomorrow. Maybe I'll know more then. Promise me not to cry. I think of you all the time and can't wait to see you. I must also bear all this. I don't want to become dependent on anyone.

A thousand kisses, Willi

Nice, August 30, 1940

Today, Saturday, is my second day here, and I am writing you this third letter for the simple reason that I think of you constantly and see you crying, but believe me when I tell you how sure I am that, as much as I would love to have you with me, it is better that you are still there. First of all, being dependent on others is not for me, and I know it would be for you a terrible feeling, even though Ernst and I were warmly welcomed by Ludwig on Friday. Henry immediately gave me some work and 400 francs, as I owed money for big expenses. I also rented a room next to Henry and Hilda for 200 francs. Monday we will go to take care of our residency permit. Supposedly this is difficult here. It is possible that I am seeing things too black! In any case, this all takes money. At noon, I go to Hilda's for lunch, and I have dinner at Mama's and sleep there too. Ludwig is angry because I don't stay for lunch as well, but I can see that that is too much to ask. Besides, I don't know his financial situation, and want to get back on my feet as soon as possible. Ernst and Gretel are using Mama's room, but I don't know if that's a good thing. At the moment, everything is going well. Lisl is here with Fritz and Ben. Her mother is here too, but Ludwig did not agree to take the old lady. Lisl wants to go to Belgium alone and have Fritz join her four weeks later. What she plans to do with her mother I do not know.

I often said how much I would like to eat your goulash with dumplings. That's what we had for dinner yesterday, and I suddenly started to cry. If I get a permit to stay in Nice, I'm sure that you will be able to stay too. In any case I would love to be with you in the room that I rented. It would be so nice not to feel so bad. Tonight I spoke with Mama and she told me that she is not happy. She would like to leave here. I must pay my debts because then I will feel better — I'm not used to being supported. The room won't cost any more when you join me, but don't expect too much. Please answer this letter to Henry at 22 Avenue Villermont chez [care of] Mme Garina. Please write me and be honest about how you are doing. I know that you are lonely. Right now, as I write to you, I am crying, and I am sitting in the corner of the room because I am ashamed. Ludwig's apartment has a living room, dining room, bedroom, bathroom, balcony, and it's very beautiful. Henry only has a little kitchen and a room where we work. Now it will be better because my room will be adjoining his. I haven't seen Nice yet, only Avenue Borriglione where Ludwig and Rosa live. Walking to their apartment is beautiful enough to paint a picture. The city is a dream city — so beautiful. When you come I want to make your life as beautiful, although it will be modest. If you knew how much I suffer, you would know what you mean to me. I count the days until you come — the hope to be with you soon is the only thing that keeps me alive. Please be brave and don't be jealous of Grete. You will be happier.

Many kisses,

Your Willi

• • •

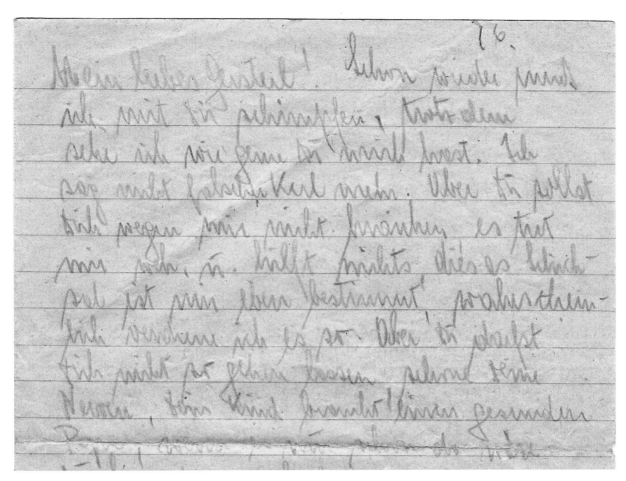

An undated letter from my mother

My dear Gerstl,

I have to scold you once again but I still see how much you love me. You should not feel bad for me. It hurts me and does not help. This fate was meant for me and I probably deserve it, but you should not let yourself go like this. Protect your nerves; the child needs a healthy papa. If only it were born already. You can believe me — my most beautiful hour will be when I have a healthy child with you near me. It won't be that much longer. Let fate then, God forbid, not take you away from me again. I am impatient also, and I can't forgive our lieutenant who told me that I qualify to be liberated, but I have to wait for the doctor to confirm that I am pregnant. Had I not known this, I would not have been so impatient. I could be with you right now, but no doctor has come yet. People do say that I have a sense of humor and am always in a happy mood; it's good that they can't see inside of me. Regarding a vacation, you imagine this is easy but this cannot happen, so forget it. Our camp is no longer a Center for Refugees, but is now an internment camp. As happy as I would be if you could be with me when I deliver, please, when the time comes, don't do it, or only if you have Proof of Loyalty with you. If I had one, I could be freed immediately, but I don't believe that Rosa can get me one. I am so happy that Hilda and Henry are so good to you and that you are with them. I hope this week to receive shoes from you — then I can go for a walk again. You know that I have the blue shoes that you bought me for my birthday. If I wear them one more time, they will be totally ripped and then I won't have any shoes at all. Otherwise, please don't spend any more; maybe only some soap, even if it's a little piece. So, dear good little Gerstl, write me diligently and then I'll be in a good mood. For today, I kiss you, unfortunately only from afar.

Your, Paula

Dearest Hilda and Henry,

I thank you for your words that always make me happy and lift my spirits. I thank you for taking Willi in so graciously. God should give that I will soon be with all of you. Otherwise I am O.K. I think a lot about you. I sing the whole day even though I would like to cry. Please write me often also.

For today, I kiss you,

Paula

.   .   .

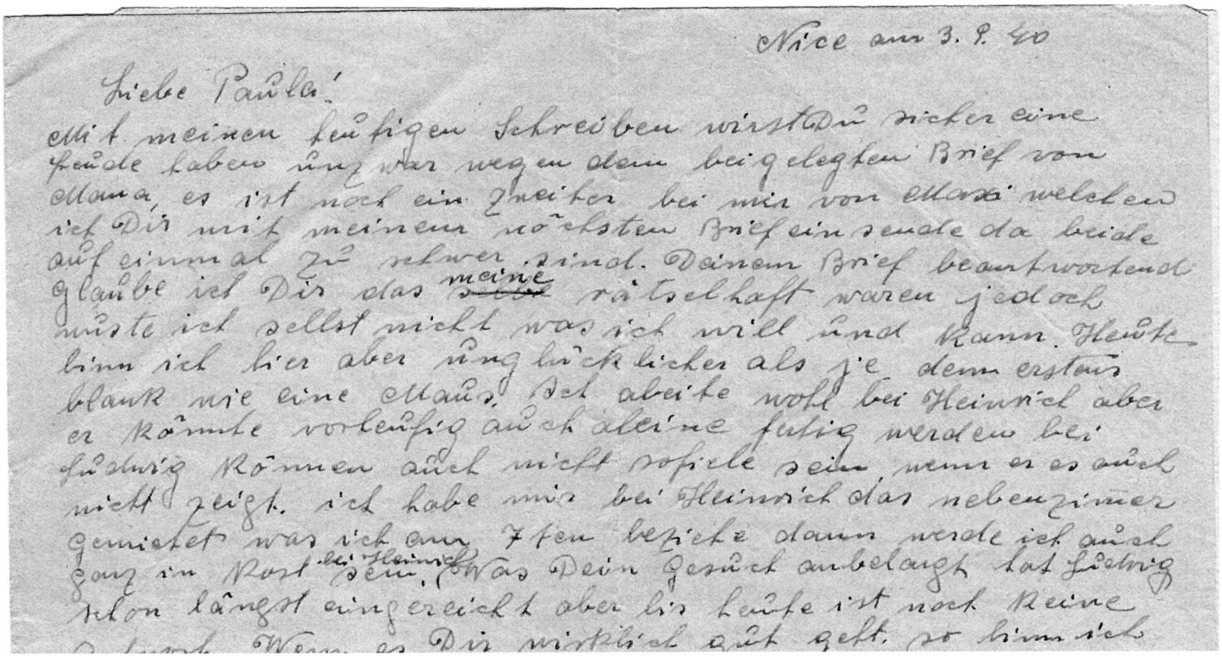

Nice am 3.9.40

Liebe Paula!

[handwritten letter in German — original script]

September 3, 1940

Dear Paula,

You will be happy with this letter today because I am enclosing one from your mother. I have one from Max too, but I will send it with my next letter. Both are too heavy to enclose. I believe you when you say that you were puzzled by my letter. I still don't know what I want or can do. Today I am unhappier than ever — I am broke as a mouse. I am working with Henry, but he could do the work himself. Too many can't be at Ludwig's either, even if he does not show it. I rented a room next to Henry's with move-in date on September 7. From that point on, I will eat at Henry's. Regarding your application, Ludwig applied a long time ago but there has been no answer to this day. If you are really doing well, I am happy that you are still there. Please ask your lieutenant if I could come and stay with you. I would like that the best. Only God knows what the future will bring. Our stay was not approved today, so Ludwig will try some other way. If you are not here before you give birth, someone for sure will come to be with you during the delivery. I also want to know if they will free you after that. I am pulling my hair out — I am the unhappiest person in the world. Try and see if I can come to you. With Mama, I don't show sadness as she would be upset. You won't believe how she has adjusted. She does not ask if we pray, we eat without wearing a head covering, and she overlooks everything. Lisl, her mother, Fritz and Ben live in a hotel, but will soon go back to Belgium because they don't have what they need to stay here. Grete feels well, but Ernst is not happy either and won't hold out this way very long. You have to have patience with a child. So you see, everything that shines is not gold. I would be the happiest if I could come to you; then we will find somewhere to go. So, dear child, I have whined to you enough in this letter. Don't worry, God has not forsaken us till now, and will continue to help us. Maybe the child will bring us luck. Maybe my depression will lift also. I am sitting here and am not paying attention to what the guests are saying. Max writes that he has a job with a locksmith and can support your mother; that's good news. Dear Paula, don't be as sad as I am, and let things happen as they will.

Everything will work out well. Ludwig is awaiting news of his application for you. Rosa will send you shoes. When you were in town, couldn't you get some there? Or did you not have money? [*Ma said she never went out of the camp; it was not allowed.*] I had asked you to send me money, but I don't think you have a dependable person to send it with. If you can't don't worry. I have good food and a good bed, but my soul aches. Why do we have to suffer so much? Did we deserve it? You will see, we will do well someday. Today I undertook making a lady's coat. Dear Paula, don't be sad that you are still there. Maybe you will be allowed to leave soon. Why do you say I can't come to you? Grete can't tell me why. I am anxious to get your next letter. Schié sent me your mother's letter. Do you have nice company? Hopefully I will be able to write you better news next time. Enough for today. Stay well and be happy. Everything will be O.K. Many kisses from your Willi who does not let a second go by without thinking of you.

• • •

Another letter from my mother.

September 15, 1940

My most beloved little Gerstl,

How do you like how endearing I can be, but only if you write me diligently and send me loving letters because I can't sleep at night. The jealousy tortures me that maybe another little Gerstl is sleeping in your double bed. I mean that as a joke. Lately, I've been very witty because of all the international men around me whom I entertain with my language skills. They even invite me to their barracks in the evening, and we eat and drink. You wouldn't recognize my sense of humor. The Czechoslovakians hold their stomach from laughter when I attempt to speak Czech. Since yesterday, I have Italian admirers — I speak almost perfect French and English, I don't even need to mention that. In a word, we will have an international child.

Unfortunately, the doctor and future prince [she too believes she's having a son] are keeping me waiting too long and you must have patience. Should you get bored, you could always pick up a little Mademoiselle. I am not jealous, and it'll make the time go faster for you. Well enough of this babbling.

I miss everybody very much. Your description of our room makes me curious. Didn't you forget a spot for our prince to sleep, a place for me to cook in, to bathe, etc.? There are so many problems but I don't want to worry about it. Hilda and Henry will have enough problems with us, don't you think? I'm urgently awaiting shoes [*she never received them*], otherwise I will have to be under house arrest, just now when I should do some serious walking. It's raining a lot, but we are already used to it. To calm you down, I have to tell you that everyone here likes me and people do everything they can for me.

I'm continuing my letter now. It's after dinner. We had vegetable soup, cold roast and a great tomato salad, wine and pudding [*better food became available when the lieutenant was replaced six weeks before Mom's liberation by a younger and kinder one*]. As you see, all is well but I miss you. You know, sometimes I think it's meant to be that we can't see each other at this time. You always said that when I'll be as big as a barrel, you will only go out with me late at night when it's dark. Well, now you have to be patient until I'm thin again. I'm really round as a ball. It's lucky that there is no big mirror here; at least I don't scare myself.

End of letter missing.

•   •   •

Barbed wire surrounded Vichy-run detention camps in southern France.
Source: *WWII A Photographic History.* David Boyle, page 204

CHAPTER VIII

Escape

JO: Papa, you were already in Nice when Mom was liberated. How did you get out of St. Cyprien?

Pop: I escaped.

JO: Tell me about it.

Pop: One day, a French official who was associated with the camp, and I don't know in what capacity because I had never seen him before, asked for a tailor. I went to see him and he gave me one of his uniforms to fix. Buttons were missing, it had a ripped seam, and it needed cleaning and pressing. I sewed on the buttons, fixed the seam, and had the uniform cleaned and pressed by a man in the camp who earned a little money by doing laundry and pressing. When I delivered the uniform, the captain was pleased, and asked how much he owed me. My answer to him was, "Nothing. What should I do with the money?" So he said, "You know what, tomorrow the Germans are coming for a transport, and all of you are going to Camp Gurs and from there to Auschwitz." So I said, "What can I do about it?" and his answer was, "Debrouillez-vous [*Fend for yourself*]." This was at the end of August 1940.

I returned to the camp and repeated this to the men in my barrack. Most of them didn't believe me, despite my efforts to convince them that I had been warned by a reputable source. I strongly recommended that we escape that night. Neue, the man who had worked with me at Kleiderhahn, thought I was crazy. He said, "Are you mad, going through France without papers? We'll end up in jail," and he refused to go. In the middle of the night, Ernie and I and four other men, including Lisl's husband, Fritz Schapira, ran to an opening in the barbed wire. There were two armed guards lying on the ground by the opening who looked like they were sleeping. Their caps were open-side up and there were coins inside. It was obvious that they wanted money, so we threw some in and ran.

JO: Were you surprised that they didn't shoot you or arrest you as you ran out?

Pop: We didn't have time to think about it. First of all, they were French, so maybe they didn't care if we got away as long as we paid our way out. Maybe they were really sleeping, or maybe the man whose uniform I fixed gave orders not to stop us. I have no idea how we got away. All I can tell you is that we ran out, and ran and ran until we could barely breathe, and reached Perpignan nine miles away. We were scared to death all the way, but we had to escape; it was risking our lives for freedom or dying in Auschwitz; we chose freedom.

JO: While walking around in the camp, did you ever discuss escaping with other internees?

Pop: Yes, it was talked about, but escaping was too dangerous and people did not want to take the chance. Besides, you couldn't get very far with a Jewish passport. Neue could have gone with us, but he was too afraid. He said that travelling in France without papers would take us from one prison to another, and what's the difference between prison in France or going to Gurs. I answered him that the difference was living in prison in France or getting gassed in Auschwitz. We would take that risk.

JO: So you knew that people were getting gassed?

Pop: Of course. There were rumors, and you either believed them or you didn't. The commandant of the camp would offer the opportunity to return to Belgium or Germany, assuring us that we would be much safer there. He was following German orders. They wanted the Jews out of the south of France and back into their hands. We later found out that those who went back ended up in Auschwitz.

JO: People believed the commandant?

Pop: Yes. Life in the camp was so unbearable, that they wanted to believe him. They were willing to take the chance.

JO: Why did you decide not to go?

Pop: Because I knew that the Germans were in Belgium and we probably would end up dead. I also knew that Ma was in a French camp so I wasn't going to go back without her.

JO: Were you scared during the escape?

Pop: We were terrified, but it was something we had to do.

JO: Were you wearing prisoner clothes?

Pop: No, no, no. We wore our own clothes.

JO: They were probably very dirty.

Pop: No. We did our laundry. Some had it done by this man I told you about.

JO: So people had money to pay him?

Pop: Some did but I didn't. I was taken prisoner in Belgium, remember? I was wearing my gold watch that day but hardly had any money on me. I sold the watch for 400 francs to Lisl's husband in the camp. It was worth three times that, but I had to have money to go to Nice.

JO: Where did he get the money to buy the watch?

Pop: He probably smuggled it in. Many people did that.

JO: Did you know what you were going to do once you got out of the camp?

Pop: We knew to go to Perpignan. That's where the railroad station was.

JO: How did you know that? You didn't know the country.

Pop: We got directions from Ludwig who wrote us from Nice. I don't know how he knew. He informed us to go to a particular restaurant in Perpignan, and he described a man who would be there to help us. This restaurant was in a hotel that housed members of the underground.

JO: Did you have this information before the officer told you that you were going to be on the next transport?

Pop: Yes.

JO: How did you find the restaurant in Perpignan?

Pop: We were walking, and a man came towards us and asked if we were from the camp. We said yes. He said, "You have to get out of here. The Garde-Mobile [*motorcycle police*] is looking for you." He led us out of that street onto another, and accompanied us to the hotel.

JO: So you think the camp reported escaped men?

Pop: Yes. We were being looked for.

JO: How did this man know you were escapees?

Pop: I don't know. Probably because of the way we looked.

JO: How did you look?

Pop: Who knows. I didn't have a mirror.

JO: I can just imagine! What happened when you got to the hotel?

Pop: We were interrogated. They had to know who we were.

JO: So it was you, Ernie, and four other men? Who were they?

Pop: Fritz was one of them. The others I don't remember. The members of the underground knew that we weren't the enemy. They hid us in the cellar for about two weeks. I don't even remember the name of the hotel.

Ma: Papa told me that Lisl was probably helpful in enabling their escape. She was a charming, beautiful woman, and she had purposely befriended one of the higher-ups of the camp. Maybe that helped.

Pop: I don't remember.

JO: What happened to her and her husband after the escape?

Ma: They returned to Belgium. A year or so later, the Gestapo came to pick them up from their apartment. I don't know where Fritz and his son Benno were at that time, but only Lisl was taken. She tried to save herself by jumping out the window, resulting in two broken legs. She lay helpless and the Gestapo dragged her into a truck headed for Auschwitz. Both she and Gretel perished there. Fritz was able to save his life and Benno's. The two eventually immigrated to the United States and settled in New York.

JO: Papa, how did you make it to Nice from Perpignan without getting caught?

Pop: Again, because I was a tailor. There was a member of the underground, a French Garde-Mobile, who needed a black suit — I don't remember if it was for a funeral or a wedding. He said that upstairs in the laundry room of the hotel there was a sewing machine and an iron, and he would bring me the fabric, thread, and whatever I needed. He wanted the suit in one week. I said yes, and assured him that I would finish it on time, even if I had to work day and night. I made the suit, and he was very satisfied. He asked what I wanted for it, and I told him that I would like a couple of Sauf-Conduits, one for me and one for my brother.

JO: What was that?

Pop: It was identification issued by the police department to gentile immigrants for traveling purposes. There was no red "J" on it, and it did not identify one's religion.

JO: Interesting that he was able to do that.

Pop: He was in the resistance, so he had connections. At first he wanted to give me only one, but I refused because I wouldn't go without Ernst. Reluctantly, he said that he would try to get two. It was a very risky thing for him to do. He told us to go to a photographer who was probably with the resistance too. We had our pictures taken, and a couple of days later, he brought us the documents. They were permits to travel by train to Marseille and Nice, and were valid for two weeks. With these in our possession, we go to the train station. We get there, we are approached by a policeman. Papers? We show him the Sauf-Conduits. He points to the train … "Get in!" We board the train, and that's how we got to Nice.

ÉTRA GERS

MINISTÈRE
DE LA
DÉFENSE NATIONALE

ÉPUBLIQUE FRANÇAISE

AUF-CONDUIT

Vala du _Vingt-six Aout 1940_
au _Neuf Septembre 1940_

N° du titre : _10.29_

M. _Kerol_ , prénoms : _Wilhelm_
Nationalité _Allemande_
Profession : _Tailleur_
Né le _1-1904_ à _Robersdorf_ Dépt _allemand_
Domicilié a _Perpignan Hotel Chapuy Fg_ Dépt _P.O._
(adresse complète)
est autorisé à se rendre à _Marseille — Nice_
chez

Signature du titulaire :
Kerol Wilhelm

Motif du déplacem _Voir Conseil_

Pièce d'identité : nature _Carte_ N° _1618_
(munie de photo timbrée)
délivrée le _11-1939_ , par _Autorités Belge_
Chemin de fer

Mode de transport autorisé :

Autorisé à conduire :
l'automobile (ou motocyclette ou bateau), marque _____ N°
(rayer le mot inutile)
Carte grise délivrée le _____ à M _____ par

Permis de conduire N° _____ délivré le _____ par
Titre délivré le _24-8-1940_
par _Capitaine Faurre Comdt Sect_

Au verso les prescriptions pour visa.)

e présent titre n'est valable qu'accompagné de la pièce d'identité désignée ci-dessus et sous réserve de se conformer aux
raires fixés e aux ordres donnés par le G. Q. G. ou les Généraux commandant les Régions traversées.
e titulaire doit pouvoir à tout moment, justifier le motif des déplacements avec pièces à l'appui.
n cas de refu par l'autorité militaire qualifiée, ce paragraphe devra être barré et la mention « refusé » portée en travers.

My father's Sauf Conduit [Safe Transit]. Uncle Ernst was granted one as well. Delivered August 24, 1940. Valid from August 26, 1940 to September 9, 1940. Authorized to travel to Marseille and Nice.

My parents reunited in Nice, September 1940

CHAPTER IX

Avenue Villermont, Nice

JO: When you got off the train in Nice, where did you go?

Pop: We went to Ludwig and Rosa's apartment.

JO: After so much time and so much suffering, what was it like to see them again?

Pop: What can I tell you! We cried, we hugged, we talked. It was unbelievable to be with our family again. We slept a lot for a couple of days. It was so nice to take a bath and sleep in a bed.

JO: What was the first thing you did when you felt stronger?

Pop: Ludwig sent us to see someone he knew who worked for the gendarmerie [*police department*]. This man would provide us with a one-month permit to stay in France.

JO: You had to have a permit to live in France?

Pop: That's right. We had to report to him every month to renew the permit. He got paid each time. After a while, the permits were extended to three months.

Ma: Do you remember how we helped people get their permits renewed with the money that I had smuggled in the pouch?

Pop: [*Chuckles*] Sure. Every month, refugees had to report to the Prefect of Police for a renewal of their permit. They had to prove that they had money to live on. Most of them did not have any, so we would loan them ours. The money was passed from family to family, and eventually would come back to us.

JO: Were you living with Tante Hilda and Uncle Henry?

Pop: For a while, but finally I had to find something for me, my wife and our child.

JO: You were sure that Ma would be liberated?

Pop: No, I was not sure, but I couldn't give up hope. I even wrote a letter to the commandant of her camp hoping to convince him to let her go. Maybe that helped because not too long after, a doctor came, signed a release, and she was allowed to leave. It was a good thing that I had found a room. It was on Avenue Villermont, in the same building where Hilda and Henry lived, which was convenient because I worked with Henry in his apartment. He was also a tailor. He had been in France over a year and had already established himself in the business.

JO: [*To Ma*] I don't understand why you were allowed to leave. You were pregnant but you were an Austrian Jew.

Ma: I'm not sure. I think it had something to do with how the prefect of the region handled the refugee situation. I would have been sent to Gurs with the other sixty Austrian/German Jews who remained, had the doctor not come when he did.

JO: How did you get to Nice?

Ma: Hilda came to pick me up. It was a long train ride, but this time, we had seats like everybody else.

JO: Papa, why didn't you go get Ma?

Pop: So that they should take me prisoner? I had escaped the camp and didn't have proper French identification.

JO: Why could Tante Hilda go?

Pop: She had immigrated to France legally, so she had proper documentation. We had escaped from Vienna and entered Belgium illegally and that made a difference.

JO: How did she get the documentation?

Pop: She had already been in France for one year. We were also legalized after you were born. I got permission to work anywhere in France because I had a French child.

JO: So Tante Hilda went alone and Uncle Henry couldn't go with her.

Pop: No, no. Traveling was too dangerous for Jewish men.

JO: Do you remember the first time you saw Ma after you reunited?

Pop: Sure.

JO: How was the reunion?

Pop: [*Chuckles*] What do I know. I don't remember. There she was with a huge stomach. She didn't look so good … not clean, torn clothing, like a person coming out of prison. What do you think I looked like when I arrived? Torn pants … the back all torn.

Ma: I hadn't seen Papa in almost five months. Of course we were happy to be together, but we both had gone through so much … the fear and the humiliation … it changed us. His voice seemed different than I remembered. I felt estranged from him. We were not the same any more.

JO: How long before you felt more comfortable?

Ma: We were never the same as we had been before the war. It scarred us permanently.

JO: Didn't my birth make a difference?

Ma: It made us very happy, but you were born three weeks after I was liberated, and taking care of a new baby adds stress, especially under our circumstances. We lived in one room and had very little privacy. We also had no time to ourselves. You became the world to Papa and I took second place. I was so weak from lack of nutrition, and so tired and nervous. I had no strength or interest in working at our relationship. Whatever it was, it was. The war was still going on, and we didn't know what tomorrow would bring.

JO: Can you tell me a little bit about my birth?

Ma: Ludwig thought I was going to have twins because my stomach was so big. The doctor said I would probably deliver sometime between the end of October to the middle of November. You were born October 19. I will never forget it. I was taken to the Louis Pasteur Hospital in Nice. I was in labor for twenty hours. A very fat nurse kept telling me to push or the baby would "mourir" [*die*]. Finally, she had to lie on me to push you out. I was in such pain, I won't ever forget it.

JO: How long were you in the hospital?

Ma: About ten days. They would keep you in a long time in those days, not like now.

JO: [*To Pop*] Do you remember the day I was born?

Pop: No.

JO: Did you go to the hospital with Ma?

Pop: No. I couldn't speak French. Hilda did all this.

JO: Do you remember when I first came home?

Pop: No. It's been forty-eight years. How can I remember! Ma will remember more because she was the one involved. I'd sew all day working to earn a little money.

JO: You don't remember anything?

Pop: [*Laughs*] I remember that you were so ugly! Ma cried when she first saw you. She thought they switched babies because she couldn't believe she had such an ugly baby. Another child was born at the same time, and he was beautiful. Months later, while taking you for a walk on the Promenade des Anglais, we saw the mother and child. He was in a brand new buggy, but he was no longer so good looking and you were beautiful.

Ma: The Jewish Committee gave us an old pram and six diapers. No one gave us anything new.

JO: They probably didn't have any money.

Ma: They had some money and could have given you a little something new. I brought you home from the hospital, and had to dress you in old rags, but I was so happy with my new baby. When I took you for a walk, people would stop and admire you regardless of the buggy. People would tell me, "Who looks at the buggy; it's the baby you look at!"

JO: Where were you living when I was born?

Pop: We lived ... where did we live? In the same apartment as Hilda and Henry ... 22 Villermont ... We rented a room ... three to four rooms were rented in that apartment. There were five floors. Mémé, Ludwig and Rosa lived somewhere else. They had a nice apartment. Ernst, Grete and Cécile lived in a hotel. I can see their room today in front of my eyes.

JO: I remember going to a beautiful house that belonged to a woman whose name was Mme Sonnenblick. Who was she?

Pop: She was a wealthy Jewish lady, a French citizen who was a friend of Hilda and Henry's. She had lived in France for many years and owned a big house surrounded by a beautiful garden. She had many fruit trees, flowers, and even chickens. We went to visit her once, and she gave you a present – one egg! She had about twenty hens, but she gave you one egg! [Laughs]

JO: She must have been ignorant about the plight of the Jewish refugees. I wonder if French Jews really understood what Hitler was doing.

Pop: Maybe not then, but eventually, when all Jews all over France were being arrested and deported, she understood.

JO: What happened to her?

Pop: I don't know.

JO: Back to Avenue Villermont. What was your room like?

MA: The owner was Madame Garino. We moved in on September 30, 1940, and lived there almost two years. Our room had a sink, so I was able to wash your diapers in it. There was no closet, just a curtain. Behind it was all I owned — the suit I wore crossing the forest. We had not been able to pay the hospital bill when you were born, and about a year later, a woman came to collect. She saw how poor we were, so we didn't have to pay.

JO: Where did you cook?

Ma: We shared Mme Garino's kitchen. Hilda and I would often cook together. I learned a little French cuisine from Mme Garino.

JO: How did you and Tante Hilda get along?

Ma: She was very helpful. She loved you very much. She did the cooking for a few months while I was busy taking care of you. I would wash diapers, feed you, take you for walks. Hilda and I would go grocery shopping together. I didn't get enough to eat, and you would cry a lot. The doctor came and said that my milk was not strong enough and that I needed to give you two additional meals consisting of regular food. Hilda would help me with your feedings. We would crush cookies and bananas and you loved it.

JO: Tante Hilda loved to tell me the "Bonbon" story. I used to call her from our balcony: "Ditta, Ditta, Ditta," and she would answer, "Qu'est-ce-que tu veux?" [*What do you want?*], and I would say, "Un bonbon [*a candy*]." Then she would bring me a candy. She loved to tell me this story.

Ma: She would have been a wonderful mother but, unfortunately, was not blessed with children.

JO: I loved her and Uncle Henry so much that I named Hilary after them. Now tell me what your life was like until the Germans invaded the south of France.

Ma: We had to register at the police station every three months. There was a severe shortage of food. The Germans took much of the food supply from France, and what was left of it had to be rationed. We would have to queue up for hours in order to get a few vegetables. I would have to get in line at five in the morning. People with children were allowed to go to the front of the line. Hundreds were behind me and sometimes food would run out and many got nothing. Grete would take Cécile. When rabbit meat was available, people with children would have priority.

JO: Did you ever get the luggage that you left with your landlady in Belgium?

Ma: Yes and no. In Nice, from September 1940 until the Germans invaded in 1942, we hoped that Germany would be defeated, that the war would end, and we could then return to our homeland as free people. Time went by, and I missed my belongings. I decided to pursue retrieving them. I had asked Fritz and Lisl Schapira, who had returned to Belgium, to look into it for us. I also wrote to our landlady, asking her to ship our things to our Nice address if they were still in her possession. We told her to keep Papa's sewing machine to cover her expenses. She wrote back informing me that Fritz had already picked everything up, and that she had kept the sewing machine for various other-than-shipping expenses. Interestingly, she also mentioned that she had opened the suitcases and boxes "to air things out."

Anyway, a big wicker trunk arrived one day that was not ours, but I assumed that that's where our possessions had been repacked. I was so happy and excited. I opened it up and couldn't believe what I saw. The content was unfamiliar and most things didn't belong to us. There were professionally cleaned and nicely pressed folded sheets and tablecloths — not ours — but when I unfurled them, I saw that they were torn. There was clothing that did not belong to us. The suits that Papa had made for me and for himself were missing, as was our crystal and other beautiful wedding gifts. Whoever packed the trunk did include Papa's patterns and tailoring books, a photo album, and a very old Megillah — a Biblical story read on Purim — that had belonged to my grandfather.

One day, I saw Grete wearing one of my blouses that she said had been given to her by her sister, Lisl. Her husband had picked up our suitcases in Belgium. Possibly when the landlady repacked our belongings after airing them out, she had mixed them up with Grete's, or maybe she had helped herself to what she liked … who knows! We never found out what happened. Soon after, the Germans invaded Nice, and we were on the run again.

JO: It would have been impossible for you to escape and take the trunk with you.

Ma: Yes, but maybe we could have left it with our friends.

JO: Who were your friends?

Pop: When we lived on Avenue Villermont, we made friends with the Ginerolis, Labress, Borellis, the Lolatas, Mr. Nanni … he was very tall, and he stuttered.

Ma: Yes, he was a good friend of Rosa and Ludwig. We also knew some Jewish people who had lived in France for many years.

JO: How long did you live on Villermont street?

Ma: Until August 1942, when Jewish refugee roundups and deportations began in the Vichy part of France.

RECETTE
DES HOSPICES CIVILS
NICE

Résidence du Comptable :
4, Place Defly, 4
Hôpital Saint-Roch
NICE

BUREAUX :
Matin : de 9 à 12 heures
Soir : de 15 à 18 h. 30

Référence à rappeler
N° 622
au 46 85 41

Compte Chèques Postaux
Receveur des Hospices – Nice
Marseille : N° 39-85

Monsieur Wilhem Gerstl

22 avenue Villermont
à Nice AM

COMMUNE DE NICE
HÔPITAL SAINT-ROCH

TAXES ET PRODUITS RECOUVRABLES
comme en Matières de Contributions Directes

Vous êtes invité à payer dans le plus bref
délai le montant des vos frais de séjour à
l'Hôpital Saint-Roch Pasteur M° 969/69
de votre femme

du 19/10/40 au 30/10/40
soit 11 journées à 6f20 = 68f20

TIMBRE QUITTANCE

A Nice, le 29 JAN 1942 194

Le Receveur,

le rapporter le présent avis en venant payer.

Unpaid hospital bill from October 19, 1940, delivered by Social Services
to my parents in 1942.

Nice, le ~~XX~~ - VI -1941

Monsieur le Préfet des Alpes Maritimes
Nice

Monsieur le Préfet,

Je soussigné Gerstl Wilhelm, né le 3-I-1904 à Kobersdorf de nationalité ex-autrichienne,

Ai l'honneur de solliciter de votre haute bienveillance la prolongation de mon séjour ainsi que celui de ma femme: Gerstl Pauline née Bender le 29-V-1909 à Vienne de nationalité ex-autrichienne;

~~Nous avons une fillette Jeanette âgée de 6 mois née à Nice.~~

Nous avons une fillette Jeanette, née à Nice âgée de 7 mois.

Nous sommes des réfugiés de Belgique en attendant notre émigration en Amérique du Nord. Nos ~~papiers~~ documents ~~pour~~ se trouvent déjà au Consulat des États Unis à Nice.

Nous sommes titulaires des récépissés délivrés à Nice en date du 6 ~~avril~~ 1941.

Dans l'attente d'une réponse favorable, veuillez agréer, Monsieur le Préfet, l'hommage de mon profond respect

Wilhelm Gerstl et femme
22 av Villermont
Nice

Letter of request to the "Prefect" asking for an extension of stay in Nice. This is a rough copy written by a French friend, as a favor to my parents who could not write in French. The request had to be made once a month at first, then the time was extended to every three months. This went on until the German invasion of the Alpes Maritimes region in 1942. Along with the request, proof had to be shown that the applicant had sufficient funds to live on.

Nice, June 7, 1941

To the Prefect [Chief Administrator] of the Maritimes Alps

Sir,

I, the undersigned William Gerstl, born January 3, 1904, in Kobersdorf, of ex-Austrian nationality, have the honor to request your high benevolence and prolong my stay, as well as my wife's, Pauline Gerstl, born Bender, April 29, 1909, in Vienna, of Austrian nationality.

We have a little girl, Jeannette, born in Nice, who is seven months old. We are refugees of Belgium waiting for our emigration to North America. Our documents are already at the United States Consulate in Nice. We have the receipts that were delivered to us in Nice on May 6, 1941.

While awaiting a favorable reply from you, please accept, Honored Sir, my deepest respect.

William Gerstl
22 Avenue Villermont, Nice

• • •

Occupied Zone and Free Zone in France 1940-1943

Marshal Henri Philippe Pétain
Head of Vichy government July 11,
1940 to August 20, 1944

In July 1940, the Vichy government of France passed the first ordinances to control Jews. Jews living in Vichy were required to have identification cards stamped with the word "Juif" [Jew.] A census located Jews and listed their addresses, jobs, and wealth. They were not permitted to change residences, and they had to inform the police about any changes in marital status. The laws enabled the regime to keep tabs on the Jews, which culminated in arrests, internments, and deportations to Nazi death camps. Roundups of 'undesirable refugees' netted 30,000 Jews.

Source: *The Holocaust Chronicle*
Louis Weber, CEO, Publications
International, Ltd., page 204.

CHAPTER X

Hotel Pompeia

JO: So what happened in August 1942?

Pop: Italy, under Mussolini, was allied with Germany and Japan. It occupied a small portion of the south of France. Germany wanted to speed up the annihilation of the Jews in the Vichy zone, and ordered Pétain to raise the monthly deportation quota. Pétain cooperated and ordered the Jewish refugees to move to ghettos to facilitate roundups and deportations. We were ordered to move from Avenue Villermont to the Hotel Pompeia. I remember … it was 5 Avenue Bardi. Ernst, Grete and Cécile moved to the Hotel Ric Rac.

Ma: I also have to add that Pétain willingly cooperated with the Nazis. He thought that if he appeased them, they would stay out of the Vichy zone. Of course, that didn't work. Anyway, the French police started massive roundups, and thousands and thousands of Jews from the Free Zone were sent to the death camps.

JO: You said that people were moved to hotels in the Nice ghetto?

Ma: They were called hotels, but they were small, old buildings with single rooms and the bathrooms were in the hallways. Our room had a two-burner cook top. Henry and Papa had rented a room as a workshop in the Avenue Villermont building in 1941, and they continued to work there. One afternoon, you were sleeping peacefully, and I was next to you taking a nap. It was a beautiful day, and all of a sudden, someone knocked at the door. It was a neighbor from upstairs, a French Jewish woman. She had come to warn me that the Germans were rounding up Jewish men for deportation. I was beside myself. Papa came home shortly after. When I told him the news, he decided to go back to Avenue Villermont and spend the night there. The next day, I went to the workshop to look for him and he was not there. I was told by someone in the building that the police had come for him, and that he and Henry had disappeared. I hurried home and on the way, I passed the outdoor market. There, standing at a fruit stand, I saw the same neighbor who had warned me the day before. She told me that she had seen Papa in the hotel an hour before, and had urged him to hide in the hallway washroom on the fourth floor because the Germans were close by.

I got back at around eleven o'clock, and the Gestapo and French police were in the building. I walked in with you in my arms and they asked me for identification. "Where is your husband," they said. I answered, "He went for bread and hasn't returned."

A man walked in who looked like Papa and you started babbling, "Papa, Papa,

Papa." They seized him and asked for identification. Lucky for him, he was French so he was dismissed. They were stone-faced and showed no emotion, no sympathy or remorse for looking to take your father away. They followed me to our room. The rucksack that I had prepared for Papa to take to the workshop was still on the bed. I said, "You see, this is my husband's bag and it's still here, so he hasn't come home." They looked around for a few minutes and walked out. I waited ten minutes, and then I went to the office with you to see if they had left. They were all gone except for one policeman who was sitting in a chair. I saw pity in his eyes, and he looked kind. We started to talk, and I told him where we came from, and that I had heard that my mother and my brother had been taken by the Nazis. I showed him their photograph, and I broke down and cried. He took out his wallet and showed me photos of his family. He told me that he was not a Nazi, that he worked for the police department and had no choice but to follow orders. At around noon, he got up and left. I don't know whether he was following orders, or he left on his own free will. Meanwhile, Uncle Ludwig sent Mme Mueller, a woman who was hiding him and Rosa, to our hotel to see if we were O.K. I told her, in my broken French, what had just happened, and that Papa was hiding upstairs in the bathroom. She said, "Go get him, and I will take him home with me." When he came down, she had me translate, "While we walk, I will talk to you, and every once in a while, nod your head and say 'oui' as though we are having a conversation." They left and I couldn't believe how lucky we were that the officer had given us this opportunity. He probably had been ordered to wait and watch for Papa so that he could take him away.

Pop: I couldn't speak French, but through Ma, I understood what I had to do. I looked Italian and that helped.

JO: Where were you when Ma couldn't find you in the Villermont building?

Pop: Henry had left the workshop to go deliver a suit to a customer in the Hotel Negresco. He went downstairs and Gineroli, who owned a grocery store on the main floor, told him not to leave the building because the Nazis were in the area looking for Jewish men. I remember this like it was yesterday. All of a sudden, six or seven police and Gestapo were pounding at the door. Gineroli grabbed Henry, pushed him into his apartment and pulled down the shades. The police ran into the building, kicking doors open on their way up. I heard them coming, so I jumped out the kitchen window into the garden before they saw me … no coat, no nothing. I ran like the devil was after me, heading to the outdoor market hoping to find Ma, but she wasn't there. I kept on running until I got to the Hotel Pompeia. As I walked in, a woman said to me, "Les boches, les boches … vite, cachez vous … 4ème étage … cabinet."

JO: The Germans, the Germans … quick, hide … fourth floor … the toilet.

Pop: I understood what she said, so I ran up to the fourth floor and locked myself in the bathroom. I stayed in there for what seemed like hours, until Ma came to get me and told me that Mrs. Mueller was downstairs waiting to take me home with her. She and I left, and we walked as casually as possible, arm in arm like a couple, and I would say "oui … oui" while she was talking to me, until we got to her apartment.

Ma: That night, three Gestapos pounded on my door yelling, "Mach auf!" [*Open up*]. I opened the door, my heart pounding so fast, I could hardly breathe. "Where is your husband?" "I don't know, he has not come home. Look, his rucksack is still here." They asked my age and your age, and looked at Mémé who was staying with me. Then they turned around and left. The same thing happened three or four nights in a row.

JO: Why was Mémé there?

Ma: Because she was sixty-six and they were not taking people over sixty yet. A week later, Mme Mueller came to me and said that she didn't have enough food for everybody. She asked me to go to the market and get some vegetables so that she could make soup. I had priority because I had a child.

Pop: She told me that I had to find another place to hide because she couldn't feed so many people. The Ginerolis, the Lolatas, and Labress volunteered to help me, and they took turns hiding me. Ma would come over with you from time to time to visit.

Ma: We were lucky because everybody at 22 Avenue Villermont liked us and were such kind, brave people. We would not have survived without them. They were risking their lives for us.

JO: How long did you continue rotating from place to place?

Pop: Months. Eventually we hid in a wine cave, Ernst, Ma and I. Gineroli had a cellar far away. He had to bring us food … I'm all mixed up. Ma will tell you the story. I remember being at Labress where I made shirts, sewed up carpeting and other things. He told me never to open the door when I was alone. He had a huge oven, and told me to crawl into it if someone knocked ... but I never had to do it. I never had to crawl into that oven. So from there I left … how did I leave? … where did I go? … Ma will tell you. You were only 22 months old and Ma was still in the hotel. She could go out on the street with you. How did I leave Labress? … the Germans occupied the city … oh yes, it was occupied by the Italians and the Italians left … I don't know. I remember like it was yesterday the shirts that I sewed for Labress …

JO: Maybe Ma can add the details that you forgot.

Pop: All she has to do is give me a couple of words and I'll remember. Right now, I don't know how I left Labress but she knows. I was there one or two months. I even remember the fabric of the shirts that I was making, and the carpets that I sewed together. I can see exactly the oven that I was supposed to crawl into. When we were with the Piccos, they were hiding this young guy, a communist who was being looked for. He was nice to me and encouraged me to keep hiding. He was part of the underground, and in a way, so was I. I couldn't work for them, but I had the same ideals. I had to hide just like they did. That communist guy was never caught, and neither was I.

JO: Ma, why did you not have to hide?

Ma: Because of you. In July, when the roundups had started, only women with children over the age of three were taken and you weren't two yet, so I was still safe.

JO: What about Grete and Cécile?

Ma: They were taken because of a mistake made by the Jewish Center in Nice, where we would get the latest information regarding Nazi activity. Flyers were routinely pinned up on bulletin boards, and people would gather around them every day to keep up with the news. This particular time, they posted that women, and children over the age of five, were being arrested. In actuality, the age was over the age of three. Neither you nor Cécile were five yet, so Grete and I went home relieved. Grete was in such a good mood that day, laughing and joking. Ernie went to see her, and begged her to bring Cécile and sleep in a cemetery with him at night, but she refused. She thought that there was nothing to worry about. In the middle of the night, the police came to the Hotel Ric Rac, took Grete and Cécile, locked them in a bus with other people who had been captured, and they were taken away. That night, I was awakened by pounding at the door. I opened it, and there stood two SS, guns and all. They entered and saw you in your crib. Cocking his head towards you, one said, "Birth certificate." I showed it to him; you were three months shy of being two, so they left. Because of you, my life was saved twice: once because I was pregnant, and now because of your age.

JO: Cécile survived. How did that happen?

Ma: The next day, it dawned on me that Cécile was born in Belgium and she might be considered a Belgian citizen. I told Ernst to have someone take her birth certificate to the police station. He asked a non-Jewish friend to do that for him; he couldn't go because he was in hiding. Upon verification, Cécile was allowed to leave. Unfortunately nothing could be done for Grete.

JO: Cécile went to visit the camp at Auschwitz a few years ago. It is now a museum

– a memorial to mankind to never forget the extent of evil and criminal acts people are capable of committing if allowed. She told me that the Nazis kept records of all victims and the books are available for viewing. From Nice, her mother was taken to Drancy. It was a hub near Paris for deportation to the death camps. She remained there until September 2, 1942, deported to Auschwitz, and she was gassed on October 2, 1942.

Ma: Those bastard Nazis! They murdered my family as well. I loved Grete very much. In spite of all our worries, we had good times together. She was not only my sister-in-law, but I considered her a good friend.

JO: For the records, Tante Rosa and Uncle Ludwig became Cécile's surrogate parents. Uncle Ernie lived close-by in Vienna, and moved to New Jersey in the 1960s. He knew that Cécile was in the best of hands and that she would be far better off staying with Tante Rosa and Uncle Ludwig. What happened to you, after Grete was taken?

Ma: In December 1942, the Italians made a deal with Germany promising to lock up the Jewish refugees and other foreigners in Italian concentration camps. We received notice in February 1943 of an obligatory transfer to Vence, a small village run by Italian military authorities. That's where we met our next benefactors, Eugene and Marguerite Francone.

My cousin Cécile and Aunt Grete in 1941

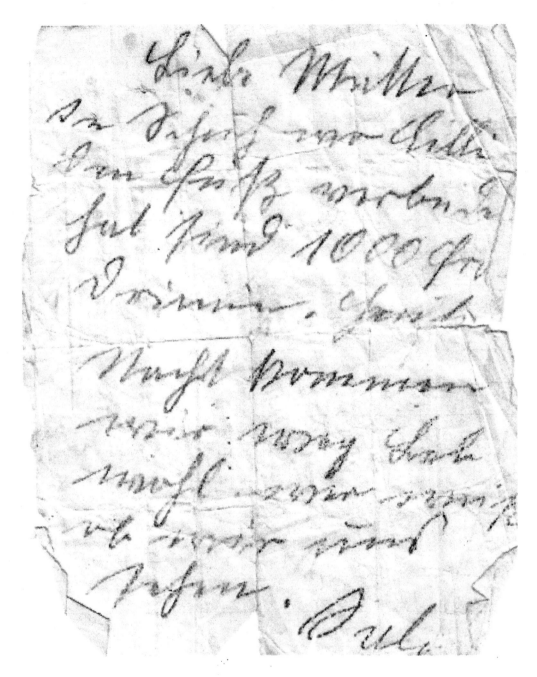

During the process of Cécile's liberation from the police station, Grete managed to find a piece of scrap paper, and wrote this note addressed to her mother. She hid it in Cécile's shoe.

Partial translation:

Dear Mother,

There is 1000 francs in Cécile's drawer..........Who knows if we will see each other again.

Grete

Téléphone : 817 - 80

NICE, le 18 décembre 1940

Attestation.

Nous certifions par la présente que Monsieur Wilhelm GERSTL, demeurant 22, avenue Villermont, à Nice, s'est mis à notre disposition pour diriger, à titre bénévole, un cours de coupe pour confection à notre Ecole de Cours Professionnels. Ce cours fonctionne depuis le début du mois de décembre à l'entière satisfaction des élèves et des dirigeants de notre Ecole.

Tout en remerciant Monsieur GERSTL vivement de son dévouement, nous espérons que nous pourrons continuer de compter sur sa précieuse collaboration.

A. Berlant
Délégué de l'ORT

My father taught tailoring in an ORT school in 1940, and the director had given him a letter of recommendation stating that he was needed there. It was not useful in the 1942 round-up.

O.R.T.
ORGANIZATION - REHABILITATION - TRAINING

December 18, 1940

ATTESTATION

We certify at this time that Mr. Wilhelm Gerstl, who lives at 22 Avenue Villermont in Nice, has volunteered to teach a course in cutting for mass production of clothing at our Professional School. This course has been functioning since the beginning of December to the fullest satisfaction of our students and school management.

We thank Mr. Gerstl for his dedication, and we hope to be able to continue counting on him for his precious collaboration.

A. Berlant
ORT delegate

Order from the Italians for obligatory transfer to Vence.

ORDER OF THE MILITARY

Nice, February 17, 1943

To: Bender, Pauline Gerstl
    5 Avenue Bardi

This communication informs the above-named of an obligatory transfer on February 22, 1943, to the locality of Vence, as the ordered designated residence.

The above-named is to present on the day of arrival to the command post CC.RR. in the area. Failure to present to the command post will provoke arrest and internment in a concentration camp.

By the order of IL TEN. COL. CAPO III S.M.
(C. Vallese)

Italian Occupation of France 1942

Source: Internet. *B'nai B'rith Europe, by Gilberte Jacaret*

In December 1942, the Italians made a deal with the Germans and promised that all the foreigners and the Jews will be locked up in Italian concentration camps …

… Prisoners were put under house arrest in Digne, Vence … St. Martin de Vesubie … The Joint (organization) gives financial help to the villages that receive Jews.

Consequently, during nine months, Jews were protected by the Italian military authorities in spite of the Germans and the Vichy government. On July 20th, 1943, the head of the Gestapo felt helpless and had to face a fact: "The zone under Italian influence, namely the Cote d'Azur, had become a promised land for the Jews in France."

At night, on September 8, 1943, the Germans took over the Italians' place.

Source: Internet. *Wikipedia, The Free Encyclopedia. Italian occupation of France during World War II, Written by Gilberte Jacaret*

Many thousands of Jews moved to the Italian zone of occupation to escape Nazi persecution in Vichy. Nearly 80% of the remaining 300,000 French Jews took refuge there after November 1942.

In January 1943 the Italians refused to cooperate with the Nazis in rounding up the Jews living in the occupied zone of France under their control, and in March prevented the Nazis from deporting Jews in their zone. German foreign minister Joachim von Ribbentrop complained to Mussolini that "Italian military circles … lack a proper understanding of the Jewish question."

However, when the Italians signed the armistice with the allies, German troops invaded the former Italian zone on September 8, 1943, and initiated brutal raids. Alois Brunner, the SS official for Jewish affairs, was placed at the head of units formed to search out Jews. Within five months, 5,000 Jews were caught and deported.

Vence, February 1943

Eugene and Marguerite Francone

CHAPTER XI

Vence Part I

JO: What was Vence like?

Ma: It was a much better place than Camp Frémont and St. Cyprien.

JO: How is that?

Ma: Although we were under house arrest at night, we were free during the day. In the camps, I slept in a stable on a cement floor, and Papa in a filthy place where disease was rampant. In Vence, we were in "Résidence Forcé [Forced Residence]." We had to live there and we were forbidden to leave, but we were treated like human beings. We had a room in a little apartment, we slept in beds, and we had food. Papa was allowed to work. We had to report to the Italians twice a day at the police station. Our identification numbers were 13 and 14. The Italians were friendly and they liked you. When we presented ourselves, you would tell them our numbers in Italian – "tredici" and "quattordici" – and they would laugh and give you a little piece of bread and jam.

We had a nine o'clock curfew every night, and the Italian authorities would make rounds to make sure no one had escaped. We had no right to own or listen to a radio. All in all, though, the Italians were not bad. They actually resisted Germany's demands for deportation of Jews. They also refused to participate in the genocide that was going on. Had we been able to go on like that until the end of the war, it wouldn't have been so bad.

Pop: I was able to work legally.

JO: How did you find a job?

Pop: I heard that a proprietor of a shop was looking for a tailor, and I applied for the position and was hired. The proprietor was Mr. Eugene Francone. I worked for him until we fled Vence six months later in September.

JO: Why did you flee?

Ma: Italy was invaded by the Allied Forces – England, Russia, and the United States. They surrendered in August 1943 and joined the Allied forces. Germany took advantage of this and invaded the Italian-occupied zone in France. They ordered the Italians to get out of Vence and take the Jews with them to a detention camp near the Italian border. Papa was a fast thinker; thanks to him we were saved. He said, "You know what, if we go with the Italians, the Germans will get us. We leave all our things here, and we go to Nice." We didn't say anything to anybody, not even Mr. Francone. We didn't want to get him into any trouble, nor did we want anybody to know what we were going to do. The night of August 30th, 1943, we got on the train and escaped to Nice.

Antibes, 1942

Emile and Lily Lasfargues, my rescuers.

CHAPTER XII

Nice Revisited

JO: When you got to Nice, where did you go?

Ma: We went directly to the Hotel Pertinax where Hilda and Henry lived. We stayed with them for a week.

JO: Where did they get extra food for three people?

Ma: Cigarettes were rationed to two packages per month per person. They would buy the cigarettes and trade them for food from people who owned a wholesale grocery store.

JO: Why did you only stay one week?

Ma: We couldn't stay longer — because it wasn't safe. The Germans had taken over the South of France, and we had disobeyed orders and escaped from Vence. We thought we might be looked for by the police. The Hotel Pertinax was located in the Jewish ghetto and was closely watched by the authorities. Besides, the five of us were in one room with only one bed. We slept on some blankets on the floor.

JO: What did you do?

Ma: Hilda had the key to an apartment that belonged to some gentile friends who had gone on vacation for a week. She was watering their plants. We stayed there a couple of days but knew that we would have to leave soon, so another plan would have to be set in motion. Hilda spoke to Mr. Gineroli who had an apartment outside of Nice. He gave us permission to stay there and we gratefully accepted. The apartment was very dirty and dark. All the blinds and windows were shut and it was so hot. The pillows and sheets were filthy. Mr. Gineroli would bring us some food late at night. You would cry because you were hungry, and I was so afraid that someone would hear you or hear our footsteps.

Pop: I remember Gineroli taking us to a cellar. Ernst was with us.

Ma: Yes. He had a second grocery store on the Place Magnan. Next to it was a stairwell that led to a cellar. It had a separate entrance. We had been in the apartment for about three weeks, and he felt that it was time to move on. The door to the cellar would have to stay unlocked at all times so that if we were discovered, he would deny that he knew us and say that we were vagrants.

JO: Was I with you?

Ma: No. It was no place for a child. Mme Labress volunteered to take you. You cried so hard when she picked you up, it broke my heart. I promised to bring you a doll.

JO: What was the cellar like?

Ma: It was a cave. Wine was made down there, so there were barrels of grapes and it smelled sour. It was dark and humid. At night, we would hear things scurrying around, maybe mice … I don't know. There were gnats and mosquitoes. The washroom was upstairs in a back hallway leading out of the store. During the day, we could use it but at night the store was locked, so Papa and Ernie used bottles.

Pop: I remember helping make the wine. I took my socks off and jumped up and down on boards to squash the grapes.

JO: Did you wash your feet first?

Pop: [*Laughs*] Of course. I would go to the store and use the washroom.

Ma: We slept on boards on a sandy floor. There were no beds down there. At eleven o'clock at night, Mr. Gineroli would bring us soup and bread. We were hungry, dirty, bored, worried about us and about you. We started to question how much longer we would have the strength to survive.

We became desperate to save your life. Your stay at Mme Labress was only temporary, and she had already mentioned that it was time to place you somewhere else. Papa and I decided that we needed to find a permanent home for you. We knew of a Jewish organization, OSE [Oeuvres de Secours aux Enfants], an underground organization that worked with convents to find hiding places for Jewish children in Christian homes. These children, however, were totally cut off from their parents, and there was a strong possibility that they would never be reunited with their families after the war, should there be any survivors. I told Rosa about our plan, and she emphatically said "absolutely no way." I will always be grateful to her for that. She made arrangements with Mme Borelli to take you for a while. I left the cave a couple of times to visit you. When I would leave, you would cry and it could be heard through open windows. Eventually, she let me know that neighbors were asking who you were, and what happened to your parents. She feared that she and her husband would be denounced. Not only would you be taken, but she would have to reveal where we were, and all of us, including them, would be imprisoned and maybe gassed in the camps. She too became anxious to have you moved to another location.

I have to backtrack to 1942. After Grete was taken, Mme Labress had told us of a childless couple, very close friends of hers, M. and Mme Lasfargues, who were willing to hide a refugee child. They lived about one hour from Nice in Antibes, and at that time we had refused because we did not want to be totally separated from you. Meanwhile, we had completely forgotten about them.

In the midst of our desperation in the cellar, I suddenly remembered the Lasfargues and their offer. I told Mr. Gineroli to ask Mme Labress to contact them. A few days later, Mr. Lasfargues came to pick you up from her house. I managed to be there too. He was such a nice man. He had blue eyes and a kind, friendly face. Every time we had to leave you with other people, you would cry and say "Mama please don't leave me; please don't give me away." Once I used the excuse that I had to go to the hospital, and you said, in German of course, "Don't go to the hospital. Please take me with you. Ich bin doch so brav! [I am so good]." [*Mom cries at this point.*] That day, you were not afraid at all; you went to Mr. Lasfargues and sat on his lap. I brought you a doll that could say "Mama" and could make peepee. You walked away holding the doll in one hand, and Mr. Lasfargues' in the other. You did not cry nor did you look back.

I gave Mr. Lasfargues the addresses of our relatives, but I told him that if we did not survive the war, we wanted him and his wife to keep you. I didn't want you to be uprooted again, even though I had a sister in England and a sister in Austria.

JO: Did you put that in writing?

Ma: No, I just said it.

JO: How long were you in the cellar?

Ma: About six weeks. We got out of there towards the end of November 1943.

Vence

Delphin Picco, circa 1940s, and Antoinette Picco, circa 1960s.

CHAPTER XIII

Vence Part II

JO: How did you get out of Mr. Gineroli's wine cellar?

Ma: I finally had to write to Mr. Francone and tell him where we were. We would pay Mr. Gineroli for our food with the little bit that we had saved from Belgium and from Papa's earnings in Nice, and had enough for about one more week. We kept hoping that the war would end and we would not have to hide any more, but that didn't happen. We offered him Papa's suit but he wouldn't take it. The only option left was selling our almost-new briefcase that was still in good shape, and the only thing of value that we possessed. I wrote a postcard to Mr. Francone with our return address on it, asking him if he would buy it from us. That's how he found out where we were.

He immediately came to Nice to find us. He was so happy to see us again. He told us that he had spoken to the police commissioner and to the mayor of Vence, and they had given permission for us to come back. There were no Germans in Vence, and he felt that we would be safe. Mr. Francone could not understand the mentality of the Nazis, and why they persecuted the Jews. That day, in the wine cellar, he gave us hope. His words were, "Come with me. I've already rented a room for you, and you will work in my store."

JO: So you fled from Vence on August 30, 1943, and returned end of November?

Ma: Yes. Getting there without getting caught was another miracle. It was tremendously risky for us and Mr. Francone. The day after we arrived, he went to the Ministry and declared Papa as a worker.

Pop: Maybe a week later, the Germans invaded Vence. A police officer who was a friend of Mr. Francone's came to warn him that they were looking for me and that, for his safety and the safety of his family, he better get rid of me.

JO: How did they know that you were in Vence?

Pop: Because I was registered. The police commissioner knew I was there, but he was limited in what he could do. I remember one day the French police came into the store to find me because the Germans wanted me for Forced Labor. There was a door hidden from view by a rack of coats. It opened into a small area within the wall designated for plumbing access. I had been instructed to hide in there if anyone came looking for me. When I saw them approaching the store, I quickly got into the wall. Mr. Francone told them that I had left Vence and had gone to Marseille.

Ma: A few days before, I was in the bakery, and the wife of the owner said to me in a much too friendly voice, "Mme Gerstl, where do you live?" I answered in French, "Oh, around here," and I got out of there as fast as I could. I was terrified. I felt that I had just encountered a spy. I told Mr. Francone what happened and he agreed that the situation had changed and we were not safe anymore. He promised that he would talk to his in-laws, Delphin and Antoinette Picco, to see if they could hide us in their attic room. Three days after my experience at the bakery, the Gestapo went looking for Papa in the store. They also went to our residence in the hotel. The owners were against the Nazis, so they said that they had no idea where we had gone, and thought that we probably had left town. We had, in fact, quietly slipped into the Piccos' attic at 5 Impasse Maurel, and "disappeared" once more.

. . .

. . .

Vence, 1942

The fountain in Vence's main square.

CHAPTER XIV

The Attic

JO: Tell me about Mr. and Mrs. Picco and their house.

Ma: They were an older couple, parents of a son, Sassan, who was in the service and stationed in the Cameroun, a French colony in Africa, and a daughter, Marguerite, who was married to Eugene Francone. They had three grandchildren, Andrée and Jean-Pierre Francone, and Jeannette Picco, Sassan's daughter. Andrée and Jean-Pierre lived in Vence, and Jeannette lived in the Cameroun.

The Piccos' home was on Impasse Maurel, a short and narrow side street that jutted off the main street and dead-ended at a small hotel surrounded by a garden. Their house was two-doors down from the hotel. Tucked behind the hotel was a building occupied by the Gestapo. It had a flat roof and German soldiers would station themselves on it and survey the surroundings through binoculars. The house had three floors. It had common walls with buildings on each side. The lower level was the basement. The main level consisted of a kitchen, bathroom, and bedrooms. A winding stairway facing the front door led to a room upstairs that was considered the attic. It was very clean and furnished with a bed, dresser, sewing machine, and a sink. On one wall, there was a window overlooking a roof a few feet down. On the other, there was a door leading to a walled balcony that faced the street, providing cross ventilation on hot summer days.

JO: What was Vence like?

Ma: Vence was a small, ancient village. It was about one hour from Nice by car, in the Maritime Alps. The ride was absolutely beautiful, but we were unable to appreciate it because we were too frightened — every corner up the mountain represented a potential threat to our lives. The village dwellings were apartments in old buildings whose stone walls showed the wear and tear of antiquity. Most buildings were adjoined, but the rooflines were all different, some high, some low, some in between, depending on the number of floors. They were covered with curved clay tiles that had been red at one time, but were now gray with age. All windows were flanked with wooden shutters. There was an old, large fountain in the middle of the main square that provided cool mountain water for the villagers and a place to do laundry. Mr. Francone's store was a few blocks from Impasse Maurel across a small park called "Place du Grand Jardin."

After we moved into the attic room, Papa continued to work for Mr. Francone using the Piccos' sewing machine. I helped him, and that's how I learned tailoring. I did the work that had to be done by hand. Mr. Francone had the best customers, including the mayor of Vence and the police commissioner. Papa was an asset to the company.

Pop: He would bring me work hidden on the bottom of Jean-Pierre's pram, with Jean-Pierre sitting on top of the pile. On the way home, if there wasn't anything to take back, Jean-Pierre, who had had a great ride sitting up high, would now be sitting much lower at the bottom. It was evident that something was going on, had anyone carefully observed the trips back and forth, but luckily we got away with it. I was paid for my work, and in turn I paid M. and Mme Picco and the Lasfargues for our keep.

JO: What did Mr. Francone do about fittings?

Pop: He would do those. I taught him what to do, and he knew a little about tailoring. His business boomed and he was very happy with my work.

JO: Was there enough food?

Ma: Food was rationed and not plentiful. It was a good thing that Mr. Francone and his wife had a farm where they grew vegetables, and they also had fruit trees. They would bring whatever they could from the farm, and Mme Picco would cook it. Sometimes we ate goat and horse meat. Good flour was not available so bread was baked with a mixture of flour and finely ground sawdust. We couldn't eat it so we would put it in a dresser drawer. We didn't want to hurt Mrs. Picco's feelings. When we left the attic, she must have found a drawer full of dry bread. Coffee was made with chicory or chickpeas, and tasted awful. I am still suffering today from stomach ailments due to those years of worry and malnutrition. But we survived, and that's what counts.

JO: I thought you said that there were no Germans in Vence.

Ma: After the Italians capitulated, the Germans came to Vence. For a while, they weren't around and we felt safe, but that changed. Our presence in the attic was a secret that no one could know, not even Mme Picco's relatives. She always said that you couldn't trust anybody, and rumors could spread. Her sister would come to the house unannounced, and if I happened to be downstairs, I would hide behind a door or in the bathroom until she left. We weren't the only ones hiding in the house. There was a young man, a member of the resistance movement against the Nazis — his name was Stalink — who worked with the underground. He was there too. One night he said to us, "You know, the Gestapo is looking for me and the house is going to be searched. You better leave for a while." A few days later, Mme Picco came upstairs at seven in the morning, and told us that we had to leave for the Francone's farmhouse immediately.

JO: She knew in advance?

Ma: Yes, because the student had told her.

JO: How did he find out?

Ma: Through the underground. Somebody denounced him and he knew about it.

JO: How did you get to the farm?

Ma: It wasn't too far and we walked. No one knew us and once we got in the street, we mingled with the people. It was very risky, but we made it. At the farm, there was a sewing machine, and we continued to work. We understood the risk that the Francones and Piccos were taking by letting us stay in their home. The whole family was in danger for hiding Jews, just as we were for being Jews. It was madness and we knew that we might have to leave. We didn't want any harm to come their way because of us. We no longer had the option of returning to Nice because the train station was closely watched by the Nazis. There was nowhere for us to go. We were desperate and lost all hope. Papa and I agreed that rather than succumb to getting caught by the Nazis and endangering the family, should there be word of a search by the Gestapo, we would commit suicide. We laid out our razor blades by the bed [*Ma starts to cry*], but God helped us again. We didn't have to go through with it. After about a week, Mme Francone came home and said that the Gestapo had searched her mother's house from top to bottom and didn't find anyone or anything suspicious. We could return to the Piccos' house.

Jean-Pierre in his pram sitting up high on the hidden clothes. Vence 1943.

Impasse Maurel, Vence 2008

The Piccos' home was at the end of this street on the left.

CHAPTER XV

1944: The Liberation

Ma: We returned from the farm to Mme Picco, but now she would leave the front door open when she left the house. The plan was that in case of a surprise search, she would say that she didn't know us, and that we entered while she was not home. She would leave us boiled potatoes and fruits and vegetables from the farm. On Sundays, sometimes we would get a sparrow or a guinea pig. Food was rationed and everybody was hungry.

Pop: Do you remember when I had that terrible tooth infection and I couldn't leave the house to go to a dentist? I was in so much pain. Mr. Francone brought all kinds of medications but it got worse and worse. I was lucky that the war ended, because I was able to go to the dentist. He pulled the tooth and told me that had I waited another few days, the infection probably would have spread and could have killed me.

Ma: How could I forget? I worried so much about you. Time went by — everyday the same. We lived in fear from one minute to the next. The weather was beautiful, but we could not go outside. We would hear bombs close by — Papa even found a piece of shrapnel* on the balcony. We worried and longed for you. We wondered how long this would go on and if we would survive. I worried about my family. I cried a lot.

Pop: Do you remember one day at five in the morning, when we heard trumpets — paratata tata, paratata tata — and we heard over a loudspeaker, "All men must report to the Place du Grand Jardin immediately. All houses will be searched. If a man is found, he will be shot and the house will be burned down."

Ma: Yes. It was July 17, 1944, a date I'll never forget because it was the anniversary of my father's death. We couldn't go to a synagogue, so the day before, I had given Mme Picco a few francs to give to the poor in his memory. We were so scared. We hurried and got dressed, went downstairs and I asked Mme Picco if Papa should go to the Place du Grand Jardin. She said no, so we went back to our room. Three hours later, at eight o'clock, Mme Francone came over, frantic. She ran upstairs and told me to get Papa out of the house. He was to jump out the window and mingle in the street. The Gestapo was next door approaching the Piccos' house.

I hurried downstairs, sat down in front of a mirror, and pretended to be getting ready for an outing. There was a loud knock at the door, and Mme Picco opened it. Two Gestapos came in. I was within their view combing my hair and putting on lipstick. They looked my way and nodded. I nodded back, smiling. My hair was long and black, and I could have passed for an Italian.

*See page 157

They addressed Mme Picco, and asked who I was. I kept quiet for fear that they would detect my German accent and question my identity. She told them that I was her cousin and that we where getting ready to go to her daughter's farm. She chitchatted with them about the farm and offered apples, which they accepted. She casually mentioned that there were two more floors, and invited these Nazis to look around if they wished. She was a pillar of strength. She spoke so confidently that they were convinced that they would find no Jews in this house. They answered, "not necessary," and left.

Papa, meanwhile, had slid down onto the roof below. He heard someone talking in the adjoining house. Fearing that he would be detected, he climbed back into the room through the window as fast as he could. He waited until the front door slammed shut, then went downstairs. When we saw him, we were shocked. We thought he had left the house. We had been on the verge of getting caught, and narrowly missed an unthinkable fate. I strongly believe that my father up in heaven helped us that day. I do believe he put in a good word for us.

Anyway, in August the Americans were fighting the Germans in France. We could hear the drone of bomber planes heading towards the coast including Antibes where you were.

JO: The Americans bombarded the harbor? Why?

Ma: Probably because it was a port and they wanted to infiltrate in order to overthrow the Germans. We could see evidence of bombs falling. I told you about the piece of shrapnel that landed on our balcony one day and Papa got it. It either came from a plane or a bomb. We lived in constant fear. Sometimes it was calm for a while, and we would be guardedly optimistic … then something would happen that would throw us into panic … and this went on time and time again for six years. While in hiding, we worried about you all the time. We prayed that you were safe with the Lasfargues. We dreaded the possibility of never seeing you again. Papa and I would discuss scenarios on how the war could end, but they were dreams, and they were not coming true. We feared death … ours… yours … all three of us … so much was going on … I don't know if we took a bath even once. We were fortunate to have a sink in our room in the attic. During our incarceration in the camps, neither Papa nor I bathed. He, at least, had the Mediterranean. Can you imagine living like that? At the Piccos', I was finally able to wash my hair. It had grown as long as yours. Actually it looked pretty nice, and when people saw me after the liberation, they told me I looked good. My body and face were swollen, I don't know from what, maybe all that fruit, but I didn't look bad. Bridges were blown up and the Americans came in further and further.

Pop: One day, at the end of August 1944, I remember Mr. Francone running into the Piccos' house. He was so excited. He said, "I don't know which flag to put up, the Russian, the French, or the American. I don't know who won the war!" [*Pop laughs.*]

Ma: We couldn't believe it. The Americans had driven the Germans out of France and France was liberated. We were alive! You were alive! We would be together once again! We wanted to run out and get you immediately, but we couldn't. We had to remain in hiding for another three weeks to protect Mr. Francone. When the Germans were looking for us in Vence in 1943 and we had disappeared into Mr. and Mrs. Picco's attic room, Mr. Francone, to protect us, had testified in writing that we had left town and gone to Marseille. He was afraid that he could still get into trouble for that. We remained out of sight until September 16th. Besides, Mme Lasfargues had asked Mr. Francone to convince us not to pick you up right away. She was now a widow and was about to lose you too. Did I tell you that Mr. Lasfargues had died?

JO: I knew that, but tell me about it anyway for the record.

Ma: One day, just before the liberation, he came to the Piccos' house to bring us news about you. The Piccos slaughtered a goat for the occasion, and served a very nice dinner. Mr. Lasfargues was in his late forties, a handsome big man, and while we ate, I could hear loud gurgling noises coming from his stomach. I don't know what illness he had, or whether the gurgling from his stomach had anything to do with it, but a few weeks later he died. Then there was the funeral, and we wondered what would happen to you now that Mme Lasfargues was left alone. Would she be able to keep you? We were helpless to rescue you.

JO: How did you find out that he died?

Ma: Mme Francone would go to Antibes once in a while to visit you and keep us apprised as to how you were doing. After one such visit, she brought back the news that Mr. Lasfargues had passed away, and that you were staying with a neighbor.

JO: Did she know for how long?

Ma: She didn't know. I think you stayed there for a week until Mme Lasfargues was able to take you back. So much more happened. I don't know what to tell you, our fear, our loneliness for you. We saw American troops passing through Vence … I saw General Eisenhower.

Anyway, back to the liberation. The war was over, but we had to remain in hiding until Mr. Francone could say that we had returned from Marseille. We were lonelier than ever and counting the days to be reunited with you.

The roof that my father had jumped on to avoid getting caught by the Gestapo.

My father found this piece of shrapnel on the floor of the balcony off the attic bedroom. Through the years, it was always stored in his sewing machine drawer.

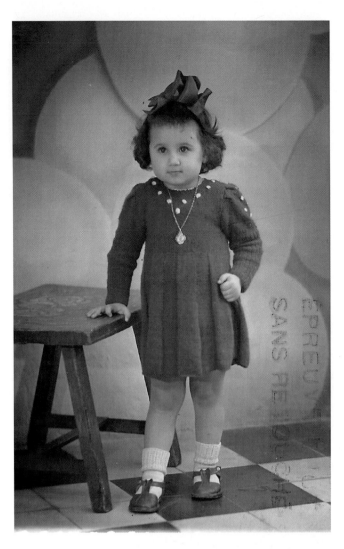

Antibes, 1943

I wore a cross while living with Emile and Lily.

In the garden with Emile.

CHAPTER XVI

Recollections of a Little Girl – My Only Memories as a Hidden Child

I am standing in a crib. I am alone and frightened. The room is small but bright. The sun is streaming in through the window. I am crying, feeling trapped in the crib, pee running down my legs.

I am in a lovely garden filled with flowers. There is a small black and white dog. I have a little red car that I can sit in and ride by pushing and pulling a T-shaped handlebar. I love the garden and the flowers.

I am in the garden with Lily and Emile, and a few people are shooting birds off the gutters. I can see skinned rabbits hanging from a line. The birds and rabbits are for our meals.

I am kneeling on a chair in front of an old, black typewriter. I am playing with the keys. There is a door and I can see into a hallway. In that hallway, two soldiers are moving about looking for something. They smell like wet wool. They are wearing yellowish-khaki-green pants tucked into leather boots almost up to their knees. What I do not remember is saying, "Es schtinkt" [it stinks.] I also do not remember them asking Lily how come I speak German, and Lily telling them that I am her niece, my father is German and in the German army, my mother is in the hospital recovering from surgery, and that she is taking care of me until my mother recovers. Lily told me that.

I am in a grotto. There is a light bulb hanging from the ceiling. Someone shuts the light off and it is very dark. We are sitting on wooden benches lining the walls. It is cold. Lily tells me to be very quiet. I hear far-away booms. I am very scared.

I am walking with Lily, and we pass a nun. Lily tells me to greet her and say "Hello, Sister." I refuse, saying she is not my sister.

I am sitting at a kitchen table with Lily, her niece Jacqueline, and some other people. We are singing French nursery rhymes.

I see two people standing in the open doorway of Lily's house. The door is thick and heavy, dark brown, and rounded at the top. These strangers are kneeling in front of me, crying, hugging me, and talking to me in a language that I do not understand. I do not know who they are. I am frightened and turn to Lily.

I am being taken away from Lily by a man who came with a truck to pick up her piano. I am in the back of the truck with the piano. I don't mind the ride because I'm having fun.

Reunion Vence Post War 1945

My father, Tantine Lily, her niece Jacqueline, my mother, and me.

CHAPTER XVII

Vence Post War

JO: When did you come to pick me up?

Ma: In September. We were so excited to see you again, hug you, kiss you, have you back with us. I wasn't sure what your reaction would be, but I imagined that you would remember us and show us some affection. Instead, you didn't know us. We were strangers to you. You were polite and interacted with us, but any mention of going back with us would bring on tears. "Jamais je quitte ma maman [I will never leave my mother!]," you said. "Je suis ta maman et voila papa [I am your mother and this is daddy]," I responded, but you ran to Lily and wrapped your arms around her. We stayed three days to give you a chance to get to know us better, but that didn't help. You kept hiding behind Lily and calling her "Maman." We were heartbroken. We had missed you so much and you had no feelings for us. You had forgotten your German. I spoke a little French, and Papa understood it somewhat and spoke a few words, but it wasn't enough to properly communicate with you. Lily asked if she could keep you a little longer, maybe a couple of weeks, to give her time to explain the situation to you so that you would understand why you would have to leave her and go home to your real mother and father. We agreed and left with a heavy heart, you can imagine.

JO: How much longer did I stay with her?

Ma: Almost two more months, until November. Lily kept postponing your departure, telling us that you weren't ready. It was agony for us. Finally, Mr. Francone, who knew how unhappy we were, made a decision without conferring with us. When Emile had passed away, Lily started selling some household items and furniture. I think she was thinking of moving. She wanted to get rid of a player piano, and Mr. Francone bought it. He wasn't in a hurry to pick it up, but when he saw how much we missed you, he took action on our behalf. One day in November, he drove up to Antibes in a pickup truck, loaded up the piano, and took you back with him. Lily was angry with us for a while because she thought it was our idea, but we knew nothing about it.

JO: I know that she got over it because she came to visit us so many times in Cannes before 1951, when we left for the United States. What happened when Mr. Francone made his surprise delivery?

Ma: I opened the door and there he was, smiling from ear to ear, holding your hand. I couldn't believe it! You were holding the doll that I gave you when you left us, and you were staring at me with your big brown eyes.

JO: I remember hiding under the kitchen table.

Ma: I couldn't wait for Papa to come home and see you. When I heard him open the front door, I said, "Papa is coming," and you ran and hid under the table. You were a little scared. It took a little time for you to feel more comfortable with us. I did the best I could to reassure you but my French was not fluent and we had difficult times. Sometimes, especially in stores when you wanted something and I said no, you became so upset that you would lie down on the ground crying and kicking, and sometimes you would try to hit me or push me.

JO: I'm sure the language barrier had something to do with it, plus the fact that I probably missed Tantine Lily. I guess I was an ill-behaved child for a while, but things straightened out, right? When did we start understanding each other better?

Ma: It took about a year. Little by little your German came back and my French improved. Because you had been moved around so much, you were insecure and you followed me everywhere. You were afraid that I would leave you again, so wherever I went, you would grab my skirt and go with me – even to the bathroom. When we went to the grocery store, I would have to pick you up and carry you. I was so weak from malnutrition, and you were heavy.

JO: By the way, where were you living when I came back?

Ma: We had moved next door to Mme Picco. There was a vacant three-room apartment, so we rented it.

JO: I remember the Catholic school I went to. It was taught by nuns. We would say a prayer every morning kneeling on our benches and facing the cross. I also remember making little bouquets of wild flowers while walking along a country road with you, and placing them at the foot of a statue of Jesus. I was exposed to Catholicism by Tantine Lily, and it stayed with me until we moved away from Vence. I gradually morphed back into my Jewishness when we reunited with our Nice family. Mémé had a lot to do with it.

Ma: We didn't discourage you. We knew that it wouldn't be a permanent situation. As a matter of fact, we instructed you never to tell anyone that you were Jewish, but to say that you were Catholic.

JO: It was customary when kids first met to ask each other what religion they were … "Are you Catholic or Protestant?" You wouldn't dare say Protestant, and Jewish didn't even come into question. France was a Catholic country and Protestants were not liked. My answer was always "Catholic." They would ask why I never went to church, so once I went because I was told that I would see angels. I did not see angels, so I was very disappointed and never went back. Anyway, we lived in Vence for a few years. The war was over so why didn't we move back to Nice where the family was?

Ma: We wanted to, but Mr. Francone's clothing business was doing well and he wanted Papa to continue working in his store. We were indebted to him and his family, and felt we should stay longer in gratitude for what they had done for us, so we stayed two more years. During that time, Mr. Francone's business grew. He had made a lot of money, and he enlarged the store. Upstairs, there was an apartment that was quite a bit roomier than where we lived on Impasse Maurel, so we moved there. He also moved the workshop that used to be in the store to an available studio apartment across the hall from us.

Pop: Yes, it was on the Place du Grand Jardin.

Ma: No, that was the entrance to the store. Our entrance was in the back on Avenue Henri Isnard.

JO: I remember a room that was a combination living room and bedroom. We only used it to sleep in because the kitchen was our favorite place. The sewing machine was in there, toys, the table for me to draw on and do homework. You would sit next to me reading the newspaper, sewing or knitting. The potbelly stove kept us warm in winter when the weather was cool. The other room had big windows facing the street. Your bed was in the room, my bed [it was actually a crib even though I was four years old], a couple of chairs, a chest of drawers and a mirror. I don't remember having company in the three years that we lived there, except Uncle Schié when he returned from Switzerland. One of the chairs had a cane seat and he sat on it. The seat cracked and ripped open, and his derrière got stuck in it. We had a good laugh, but I remember how upset you were because the furniture did not belong to us.

Ma: Nothing belonged to us.

JO: I also remember a blue balloon that you bought for me from a vendor on the street. I loved it so much and kept it for months. It floated and floated until it shriveled up and died. The balloon, a porcelain doll with paper hair, a very small white furry stuffed dog, and a ball that Uncle Schié brought from Switzerland were my only toys.

Ma: [*Laughs*] That poor ball. It was a large, beautiful rubber ball. I crocheted a special bag for you to carry it to the park. Do you remember what you did to it?

JO: I sure do. I was rolling it around against the wall with my forehead, and suddenly I wondered what was inside. I took a straight pin and poked a hole in it. It slowly deflated and no longer bounced. You took it to a bicycle shop and they patched the hole, but it was never the same.

Ma: It was too bad because we didn't have any money to buy you another one. You had gotten the doll from Tantine Lily, and the dog from the Francones.

JO: I did do some silly things over the years, but I straightened out pretty well considering my behavior when I first returned to you. I remember getting the Croix d'Honeur [Medal of Honor] from the nuns for being the best student of the week, and as a reward, you bought me a little blackboard that was made of a white plastic material. You could write on it with a pencil and erase it. I wanted it so much and I was so happy and proud of having earned it.

Ma: What else do you remember about Vence?

JO: I remember being nauseous a lot. I don't know why because there was nothing wrong with me. It might have been anxiety. I also remember the day I had my tonsils out. You told me that we were going to the shoe store to buy shoes, and meanwhile you took me to an old building where we waited in a room that had no furniture in it, except a few chairs. I was moved into another room without you, wrapped tightly in a sheet like a mummy, and placed on a man's lap. A doctor sat across from him and placed a helmet that looked like a deepsea diver's gear over my head. It was used to administer ether. When I got home, you got ice from the butcher shop and you crushed it into ice chips that I sucked to ease the pain in my throat. There was no ice cream at the time. I also remember developing a very high fever and hallucinating.

Ma: You developed an infection from the operation.

JO: Where you happy in Vence?

Ma: No. Everyone knew we were Jews. I continued to feel persecuted even though the war was over. We wanted to leave but couldn't yet. The time was not right.

Andrée, Jean-Pierre and I at a community
children's costume party. Vence 1946.

My mother, my father and I are reunited forever. Vence, France, post-war 1945.

William Gerstl

Job Search

Vence, March 13, 1947

Dear Sir,

I am honored to have the opportunity to offer my services to you as pattern designer/cutter specializing in English design for men and women.

I am of Austrian origin, passed my exams as Master Tailor in Vienna, and worked in Hungary for a while.

From 1933 to 1938, I was head pattern designer/cutter in the leading house of confection, "House of Kleiderhahn", Vienna XIV, Sparkassenplatz. I take the liberty to enclose a translated version of the letter of recommendation that I received when I left the company. The original is in my possession and is at your disposal, should you wish to see it.

In 1938, due to circumstances of the war, I left Vienna and settled in France, where I have been working since 1943 as a cutter in Vence. Because the village is very small, I would like a change and hope to find a position as a cutter in a big company in Nice, preferably yours as I know its reputation.

I would very much appreciate a response from you as soon as possible.

Sincerely yours,

William Gerstl
3 Av. Henri Isnard
Vence, A.M.

CHAPTER XVIII

A New Beginning

JO: So it's 1947, France was liberated on August 15, 1944, and you are still in Vence waiting for visas to go to the United States.

Ma: Yes, we still don't have visas and there is no future for us in Vence. Two years before, we had told Mr. Francone that we couldn't live on the little money that Papa was earning even though the apartment was free, so he gave Papa a contract for a year with a bigger salary. He also would bring us vegetables from the farm and clothes that Andrée had outgrown. But we knew that that was not a future for us. I had told him that Papa was a pattern maker and custom tailor and could earn a lot more money elsewhere, but we would remain for two more years in gratitude to him and his family. That's when he gave Papa the contract with a salary of 20,000 francs. I still have that contract. Time went by. Everything got more and more expensive and we had to ask for a raise again. This time, he said he couldn't do it. We understood that, but we also had to plan a future for you and wanted the opportunity to make a better life for ourselves. Finally, I put an ad in a Nice newspaper stating that a tailor is looking for a position, and I got ten responses. I sent out resumes to these ten companies, and Papa got seven offers. We really wanted to go to Nice because Mémé and the whole family were there, but in Nice, even though Papa would have earned much more than at Mr. Francone's, housing was very expensive. Meanwhile ... what was his name, Willy?

Pop: Who?

Ma: The owner of Miami Tailleur....

Pop: Agarrat.

Ma: Yes, Mr. Agarrat. I sent him a resumé, and he responded. He offered Papa a position in his store in Cannes. Besides Papa's salary, the position would include the rent for an apartment. It was an offer we couldn't refuse. We were very sad to leave Mr. Francone and his family. They saved our lives, and we tried to do as much as we could for them too. We stayed the two years, even though we couldn't wait to leave Vence and start over again in a bigger city. We were grateful and we felt we owed it to them.

Pop: While we were hidden, I was paid for my work, but I did contribute to Mme Picco and the Lasfargues for our keep. After the war, I started saving a little, but it wasn't enough.

JO: You were such a wonderful tailor, I'm sure you helped make his business successful.

Pop: I think so. He was a nice man, Mr. Francone.

Ma: Very nice. When he could, he would bring Papa a package of cigarettes. But he was angry that we were leaving.

Pop: Once he brought me a whole box of cigarettes … maybe thirty packs.

JO: You must have been in heaven.

Pop: You can imagine. At that time you could only get them with an alimentary card. Tante Hilda would trade them for food. One time, when we were hidden, he noticed that I was in a very bad mood. He said to me, "Why are you sad?" and I said, "I don't even have a cigarette. I work and don't even have a cigarette." He said, "You don't have cigarettes? I'll see what I can do." And that's when he came, the next day, with that box.

JO: Where did he get them?

Ma: He had connections with German soldiers who were his customers. They would get fabric, clothing and other things from him at cheap prices.

Pop: I didn't trust my eyes … a huge box of cigarettes!

Ma: It wasn't that big. You are exaggerating.

Pop: Yes, it was a suitcase full.

Ma: O.K., O.K., forget about it. I'll tell you something, at that time you had to have tickets to purchase things. There was very little to buy, no clothes, no fabric, etc. Eventually, when more goods became available, he converted the store from a clothing store to a small department store. He sold dishes, fabrics, souvenirs, and much more.

JO: He was quite a businessman, wasn't he.

Pop: Too much, too much. He bought more stores, and eventually a restaurant and a hotel. Unfortunately, he ended up bankrupt.

JO: That was much later when we lived in the United States.

Ma: Yes. After the war, he didn't have as many customers, some of Papa's customers didn't come back, there was inflation … he got sick …

Pop: Yes, we were already in the United States. How was it that I went to his grave once?

Ma: We went on a trip to Europe in the 1960s, and stopped in Vence to see Mme Picco and Mme Francone. We all went to the cemetery to visit his grave.

JO: You mean he died before Mme Picco?

Ma: He was around fifty when he died. He was about the same age as Papa because Mme Francone was about my age. We were all young then.

Pop: He was a nice man.

Ma: He was nice. He couldn't understand why Jews were being persecuted. He would say that this was an atrocity to human beings. He knew us well. We lived with his in-laws for one year, Papa worked for him before we fled Vence, while we hid with the Piccos, and two more years after the war. He was appalled at the inhumanity and cruelty of the Nazis.

JO: So you left Vence in 1947 and moved to Cannes?

Ma: Not immediately. We lived in Nice for five months. We rented a room in a lovely house with a beautiful garden. The owner was Mme Raschen, and the house was on the Avenue des Acacias.

JO: I remember the garden. I planted a potato once, and would dig it up every couple of days to see if it was growing.

Ma: You were seven years old and fortunately didn't understand the extent of our worries. Meanwhile, Papa was hired by Miami Tailleur in Cannes. We found a nice apartment overlooking the Mediterranean. The wife of the director of the store went with me to look it over. I thought she was so nice, but actually she was very jealous that we, as Jews, got such a nice place to live. Her apartment was over the store downtown. They were anti-Semites.

Everything would have been wonderful in Cannes, but we had no one, no friends, no family, very little money. We were surrounded by people we didn't trust, everything got more and more expensive, and we didn't see a future for you or for us. We wanted to go to the U.S. We were packed to go in 1946 when we were still in Vence, but the visas fell through … so much more…

You know, I am so tired I can't speak anymore. Don't be upset with me, but we'll finish some other time.

Pop: Maybe one day.

We left Europe on November 13, 1951, and reached the shores of
the United States on November 27, 1951.

United States Senate

COMMITTEE ON
LABOR AND PUBLIC WELFARE

May 18, 1959

Miss Jeannette Gerstl
3323 Sturtevant
Detroit 6, Michigan

Dear Miss Gerstl:

I understand you have recently become an American
citizen.

It is indeed a pleasure to welcome you and to wish
you every success in your adopted country. There
are, as you realize, many responsibilities as well
as privileges connected with American citizenship;
but you probably understand this better than many
native-born Americans.

In any event, I want to offer my heartiest congratulations and my services as your Senator in any way
that is possible.

Sincerely,

Pat. McNamara

PAT. McNAMARA, U.S.S.

I am welcomed as a citizen.

Reunion of Mme Picco and my father in Vence 1965.
They are standing on the balcony off the attic room.

LETTERS

Lily to Jeannette

Ma and I corresponded with Tantine Lily until her death in the late 1960s. I have many letters, too many to include in this book, so I have chosen the five that I cherish most.

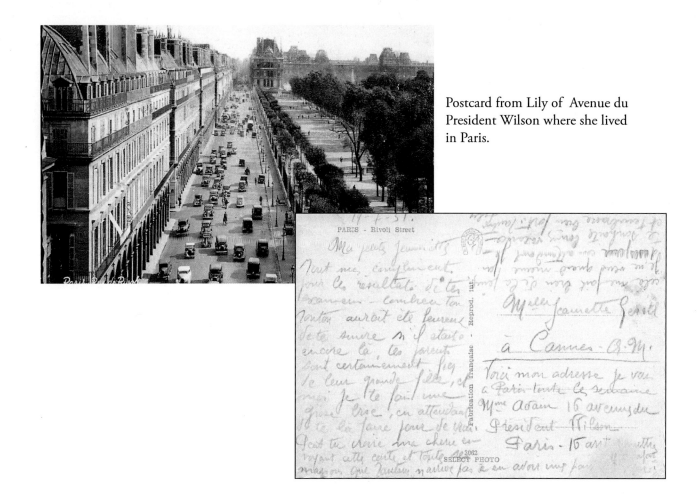

Postcard from Lily of Avenue du President Wilson where she lived in Paris.

Miss Jeannette Gerstl
In Cannes, Maritime Alps

July 19, 1951

My little Jeannette, [*I was 10*]

All my compliments on the results of your exams. How your Uncle Emile would have loved to follow your accomplishments, had he been here. Your parents are certainly proud of their big daughter, and me, I send you a big kiss until I can do that in person. Can you believe, my darling, when you look at this postcard with all the big apartment buildings, that your auntie cannot achieve to get an apartment of her own? It makes me very sad, but I do not want to give up hope. Meanwhile, I wish you a good vacation. Big kisses,

Tantine Lily

My Paris address is
16 Avenue du President Wilson
Paris, 16th district

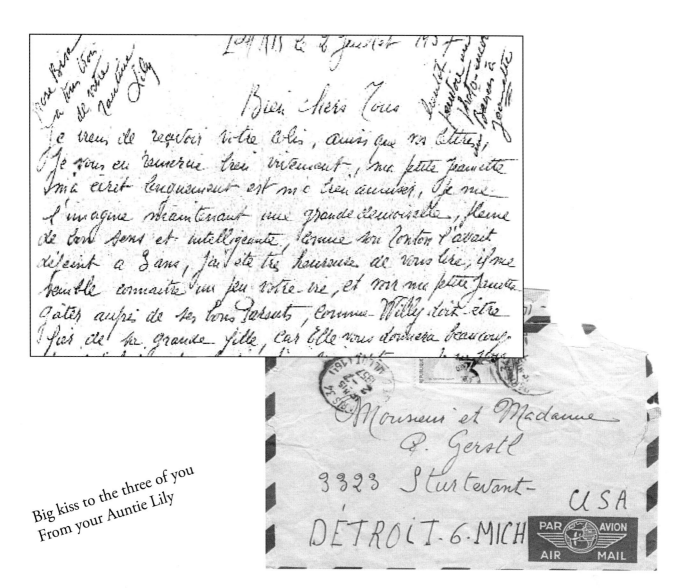

Big kiss to the three of you
From your Auntie Lily

Soon I will send another photo.
Kisses to Jeannette

Paris, July 2, 1957 [*I was 17*]

Dear all,

I have just received your package and your letters. I thank you very much for this. My little Jeannette wrote me a long letter and it really amused me. I imagine her now to be a young mademoiselle, sensible and intelligent, as her Tonton Emile described her at the age of three. I was happy to read your letters. It feels like I know a little about your life, and I see my little Jeannette well loved by her good parents. Willy must be so proud of his big daughter, because she will give you much satisfaction in life, I am certain. I do not see in my family any of my nieces around her age as quick of wit as that little one. It is true that she is in good hands and that often children turn out the way they are brought up. I showed her little letter to all my friends and I am proud of it, because here, you know Paula, all my friends know you, as I speak so much about you and my little one, and my whole family loves you. Aren't we related a little in our affections? My strongest wish would be that I should have the immense joy to see you again. We are so far from each other. Anyway, the good Lord will permit us this, I am sure.

[The rest of the letter relates to family events.]

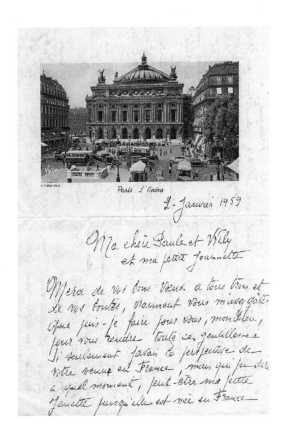

Paris, 16th District
January 2, 1959 [*I was 18*]

My dear Paula and Willy, and my little Jeannette,

Thank you for your good wishes and your kindness, you have really spoiled me. What can I do for you, my God, to return all the nice things you do for me. If only I could look forward to a visit from you to France, but who knows when. Maybe my little Jeannette, because she was born in France and wants to become a French teacher, she could maybe take a trip to Paris and stay with me a while. Anyway, I am not giving up hope that my dream will be realized. Meanwhile I wish all three of you good health, happiness and prosperity, I hope that your niece and baby are well. Now your sister is not as alone, not like me who will never have this joy …

My little Jeannette, you ask me if Jacqueline remembers you. You can believe that she does, and she loves you very much. She often reminds me of your little mannerisms because you were so fine and delicate, although very tiny, and you often made us laugh. She sends you many kisses. Before concluding this letter, I must thank you very much and let you know how delicious the candy is. As Jeannette writes to me, "think of me every time you eat a candy." My little sweetheart, Tantine would have loved to keep you and I think of you often, you know, and would love to have you near me. Tell me in your next letter about your New Year's Eve dancing party and what you wore – Auntie is curious, you will say!

I am leaving you now to mail my letter this evening. Hugs and kisses to all three of you. Hope to read you soon. Kisses.

Tantine Lily
Big kiss to Jeannette
Regards to everyone in your family

Paris, March 7, 1962 [*I was 21*]

Dear all,

I received your letter, dear Paula, and am surprised that you tell me that you have not received any news from me since you sent me your wishes accompanied by your generous gift. I sent you a card acknowledging receipt and thanking you for the gift. I sent it two days prior to my departure to Fergnier. I had the opportunity of finding a replacement for three weeks, a friend of mine who was available. This permitted me to go visit my poor nephew who is slowly fading away. This is so sad because he is totally lucid and you can hear him with a faded voice giving advice and make his recommendations to the children and to his dear wife, who does not want to leave his side, truly how sad this is. I wonder why, when doctors declare the patient incurable, they still want to prolong life. He is a skeleton. As long as his heart can take it, they do blood and serum transfusions to prolong his life. My niece, Lily is very good to her parents, and her husband as well; the other girls are younger and don't understand the situation as much.

So my little Jeannette will soon have her baby. How much more waiting time, my dear Paula, for you to become a happy "Mamie" [*Sheldon was born on March 24, 1962*]. Willy must be happy as well. I see in my thoughts the joy both of you must feel. They started early, that's true, but it's better that way, than to remain a whole life as I did, without having known the joy of being a mother. Don't you ever have any family or friend who would come from a country like Cécile's, or from the Riviera, who might come through Paris and I would have the pleasure of welcoming them to my home? I have a fairly nice home and could even house whoever would come to see me. I would be so happy to have a visit from you. Maybe Jeannette and her husband will surprise me one day.

I don't know how my niece will handle things after the death of her poor husband, with her three daughters. Maybe she'll come to me for a while. I had someone replace me for about one month after the first of the year to go visit them. My brother, the one you met, also is not doing well. He cannot move and soon he will be completely paralyzed. What a sad illness is his. I am stopping. What a sad letter I am sending you. Please forgive me because I am so sad and when I write to you, I feel as though you are near me. Maybe when you receive this letter, you will have received my card. Send me news and when Jeannette has her baby, she should not do anything careless. I kiss her dearly as well as her husband. Tell me his name in French please.

For you two, affectionate kisses. It is very cold in Paris. How is the weather in Detroit?

Your Tantine Lily
Big kiss to the three little ones

Paris, March 2, 1967 [*I was 26*]

Dear all,

How could you have thought for one instant, my dear Paula, that I had bad thoughts about you. A person can have great sorrow and not want to torment those she loves. That was my case. It has been eleven years that I have not returned to Nice, even though my friends, Labress, ask me to come constantly. I think that when I will go there, it will be for the big voyage…

I had a great shock at my poor sister's untimely death, brutally and in two hours. Six months later it was my brother, the one you knew. I had a nervous depression and an infarct after a surgery for an umbilical hernia, loss of memory, and having such a huge responsibility in this large apartment building, getting up early and going to bed late, and most of all never to complain because I knew that no one in my family could come to me.

There also was a chimney fire in this huge apartment building. This is not a single woman's work. Anyway, I gave a lot of myself and finally became ill. I am grateful that everyone around me is nice towards me. Luckily, I almost have a daughter whose name is Janette [probably a friend in Paris]. Today I feel better and I was well cared for. I did not write my problems to you knowing too well that everyone has his/her problems in life. Therefore, my dear Paula, do not have any bad thoughts towards me.

I was very happy with Jeannette's letter and the picture of her three beautiful children. Her husband appears gentle and friendly. Jeannette looks like you, especially her hair, when I knew you approximately 23 years ago.

I kiss you warmly big and small, and mostly do not think that I forgot you. I would have liked to go to Nice last year and maybe visit Willy's brother. I am enclosing a few old photographs and the necklace as a souvenir to Jeannette, because today I am here, and tomorrow I do not know what will become of me.

Big kiss to all, Lily

[***Note: a birthday card is included with the letter***]

My little Jeannette,

I do not remember the date of your birthday but I know that it's in March [*it's in October but she forgot*]. Happy birthday for 1967 and a big kiss, Tantine Lily

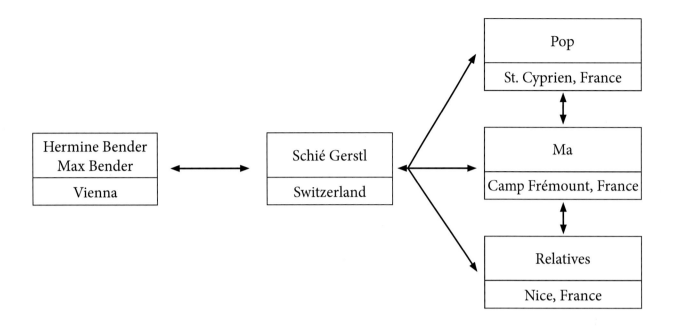

CORRESPONDENCE

Max Bender and Hermine Bender via Uncle Schié in Switzerland, to Camp Frémont, Camp St. Cyprien, and Nice

After Austria's union with Germany, Austrians could no longer send mail to the Allied countries, including France. Switzerland was officially neutral during WWII. The postal systems between that country and Nazi Germany/Austria were not affected. My father's brother, Schié, had fled Vienna before my parents, and had settled in Switzerland. He sent my father his address, and my mother passed it on to my grandmother Hermine and my uncle Max. They had remained in Vienna, and when my parents ended up in the detention camps in France, and later on in Nice, they were able to correspond via Schié in Switzerland. He would open the letter, add a few words, and send it on to the designated recipient. Numerous family members in Vienna would add a note to my grandmother's writings as well. The correspondence continued in this manner until my grandmother and uncle were taken from their home and deported to Latvia where they lost their lives.

Mail from Austria was censored, as evidenced by tops of letters being cut off. It was, therefore, necessary to be cautious and not write anything negative about conditions there.

I only included pertinent snippets of the letters. I excluded redundant news about family members and friends I did not know.

This letter addressed to my mother, from Max and my grandmother in Vienna, shows the journey of the letter. It is sent to Uncle Schié in Swizerland, and he forwards it to his mother in Nice, France, for reasons explained in his note below. The notes in green ink are written by Max: one to my mother and one to Schié. The second note in black is from my grandmother to Schié. The last note is from Schié to his mother [my paternal grandmother] in Nice.

Dear Mama,

Please give Paula this letter when she arrives in Nice. I got a letter from her asking me to forward her mother's mail to you because she does not know how long she is to remain in the camp.

Kisses to all of you,
Schié

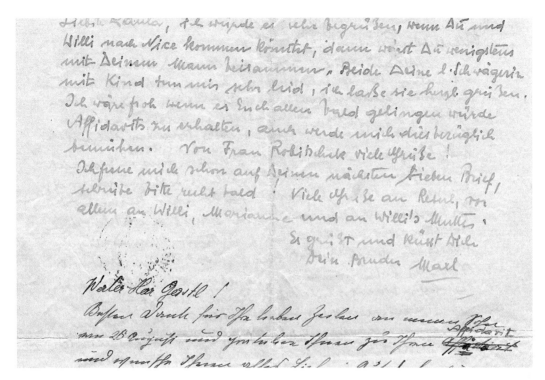

Letter from my grandmother to my mother, probably written in late August or September 1940, when she received the news that my mother was pregnant. The top of the letter was cut off [censored] before it reached my mother.

My darling beloved Paulinkel,

The content of your letter put me in such a good mood because that rare pleasure of finally having a grandchild will soon, with God's help, be realized. You waited a long time, but this new little citizen will be welcomed with double the happiness. I pray with all my heart that God will, in that difficult hour and in a strange country, protect and shelter you. That child will mean everything to you, and will help you forget all that is bad and evil. Keep your head up my dear child. Nothing but good can happen to you because those who so respected and were so good to their parents as you and Willi, what bad can happen to them? I am happy that dear Willi and his family already are in Nice because you will also have the opportunity to get there. Today I went to visit Mrs. Korn* and she was very happy to receive regards from her husband. She is a lovely lady and she is doing O.K. She thanks you for your intervention and wishes you well. She sends her love to her husband. I wrote to Willi today.

So, my dear child, be happy and optimistic. Everything will be well again and you will be together with your beloved husband once more. I kiss you and hug you a thousand times.

Your loyal and loving Mother.

P.S. For the coming new year, best wishes for good health. The rest will happen. Lots of luck. Max comes home from work very late every night. He can only write on Sundays, and he will do so soon. He sends his love and regards and best wishes.

*Wife of Dr. Henri Korn who wrote the beautiful congratulatory letter from Gurs to my mother.

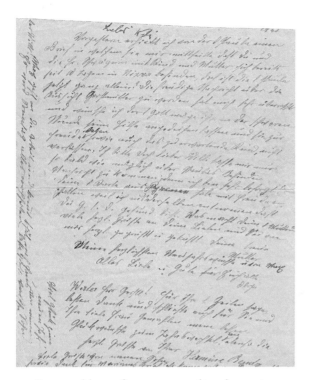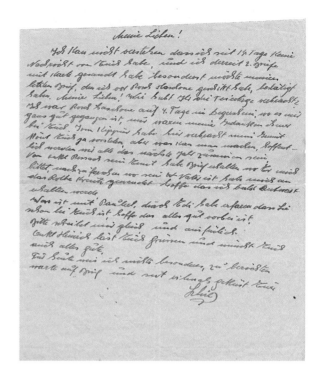

Censored letter from my grandmother written to my father in 1940. Backside: a note from Uncle Schié.

Dear Willi,

The day before yesterday I received a letter from Paula and she informs me that you and your sister-in-law and her child have been in Nice for ten days. Paula is now alone. The wonderful news about becoming a grandmother surprised me and I pray that the dear Lord will help her in that difficult hour and will bring her and all of you the happiness that you so deserve. May He bless and protect the child as well.

Please, dear Willi, let me know as soon as possible about Paula's condition. I am very worried. I was very happy to receive your card from St. Cyprien because it brought me the news that you are healthy. How is your mother?

Many regards to your loved ones. I send you much love and kisses,

Your loyal Mother

Note to Schié:

Dear Mr. Gerstl,

Many thanks for your kind words. I am enclosing my best wishes for the New Year to you and your wife. Regards from my son who thanks you for Marianne's letter. He can only write on Sunday. He works hard and comes home late.

Hermine Bender

Note added by Schié to the family in Nice:

My dear ones,

I can't understand why I haven't heard from you in two weeks. I sent you two letters and one postcard which you have not acknowledged. My dear ones, how were your holidays? My thoughts have been with you. My mood was especially bad on Yom Kippur, you can imagine. Let's hope that we will all be together next year. I got a letter from Uncle Pesach asking me to see if I can find out where his father is. I contacted the Red Cross and hope that I'll get an answer soon.

Willi, what's new with Paula? I heard through Hilda's brother, Edi, that she is with you now. Please write me a detailed letter immediately.

Schié

•　•　•

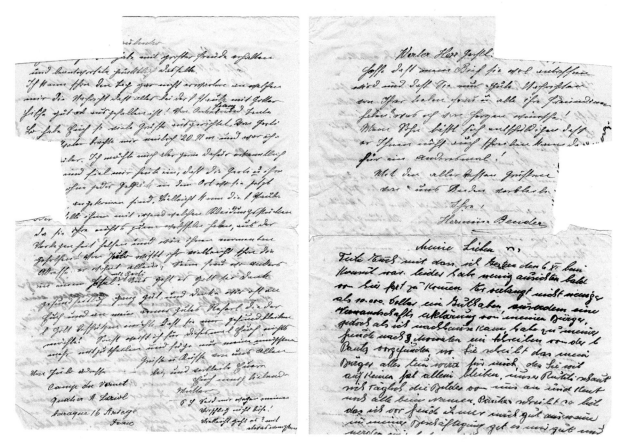

Censored letter from my grandmother to my mother and Uncle Schié, with additional note from Uncle Schié.

I was so pleased with your card, and it made me especially happy. I can't wait for the day when I receive the news that, with God's help, everything worked out well with the birth. I sent regards from you to Uncle Franz and aunt Lou. Gerti brought me 20 Reichmarks. I would like to show her my gratitude. Maybe Willi can help with some kind of clothing as they do not have a change of clothes; it would help me and them. You might already know Uncle Julio's address [Camp du Vernet, Quartier A Lariol, Baraque 16, Ariege, France.] His wife rents a room in a hotel close to the camp. We are well and we think often of you and my poor, good Rési — God should protect her and keep her healthy.

Best regards and kisses,
Your loving mother

P.S. Don't be mad at me about my proposition! Maybe it can work? Helping out with something.

Note to Schié:

Dear Mr. Gerstl,

I hope my letter finds you well and that you are receiving good news from your wife in England. My son apologizes that he cannot write today. Best regards from both of us. Hermine Bender

Note from Schié:

My dear ones,

I am informing you that yesterday, November 11, I went to the consulat. Unfortunately I have little chance to get away from here. He is asking no less than $10,000, and an affirmation of character from a sponsor. As I got home, after three months of not hearing from her, I found a letter from Paula [Gutstein]. She says that my sponsor will do everything possible for me. She also says that our little Ruthie looks at our photos daily, and still knows us all by name. Paula writes so lovingly that I cried from happiness. My job is fine.

Kisses,

Schié

. . .

Letter from Uncle Max, with notes from my grandmother and Uncle Schié, probably written in late September 1940. Top was cut off.

My most beloved Paula,

First of all I wish you and dear Willi and his entire family best wishes for our holidays. May the dear Lord protect you in every way and keep you healthy. Mama, Mimi, Hans and I are very concerned and worried about your condition, and hope to hear from you soon that you have become a happy new Mom and are being well taken care of at your mother-in-law's, close to your husband.

I have little time for myself, as I work at a new job in a factory that makes farming machines. I only have a few hours off on Sunday afternoons; that's when I rest from that heavy work. Please don't be angry because I write so little and so seldom. I earn decent wages and can support Mama. I am healthy except for a small injury to my foot that happened at work. It is almost healed. Phillip was here the day before yesterday with good news from Rési. I received mail, thank God, from Marianne as well. Regards from Nori, Ruthi, Ernst and parents. The children came to see us Sunday. Mr. Ettinger sends his regards and thanks you for your help in getting news from his daughter, Irene, who is in Antwerp. I often visit Marianne's mother, and she sends her regards to you and Willi every time. I can't wait for your next letter.

Again, best wishes to you, Willi and his mother, and Willi's brothers and sisters.

Kisses, Your brother Max

My grandmother adds a note:

My most beloved Paulinkel,

Through your brother-in-law, Mr. Gerstl, we received some news about you and I am assuming that with God's help, everything went well and that you and your darling child are well and will soon get to Nice [*she thought that Ma had given birth in the camp*]. I wish you with all my heart everything good and that the good Lord protect you wherever you go and grace you with the best. Please, if possible, inform us as to your condition. Meanwhile I kiss you and hug you in spirit.

Your ever-loving and faithful,

Mother

·   ·   ·

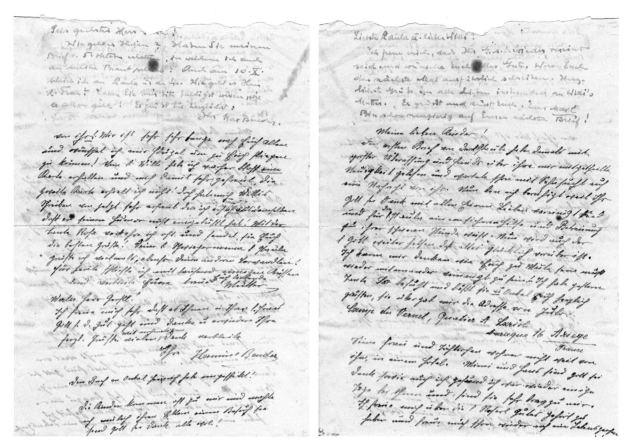

Censored letter from Max and my grandmother, probably written in mid-October. The top of the letter was torn off.

Note from Max:

Dearest Paula and dear Willi,

I am happy that you and Willi are, thank God, reunited, and wish you the best. I will write a more detailed letter next time. Best regards to your family, especially to Willi's mother. Best regards and kisses to you, Max

I can't wait to read your next letter.

Note from Max to Schié:

Very Honorable Mr. Gerstl,

How are you? Did you receive my letter from the 5th of October, in which I also added a note to my fiancée? I also wrote on October 10th to Paula and to you. How is your wife? Please let me know soon how everyone is doing.

Best regards,

Max Bender

Note from my grandmother:

My beloved children,

I read your last letter with much surprise and happiness over the news that Paula is finally in Nice, and am awaiting with great longing for more news. Now I feel more relaxed because I know that you are among family and that will be a big help and moral support during that trying hour. God will also continue to watch over you and everything will work out well. I can imagine how happy you must be to be together again. Mimi and Hans are doing well. I was there for a few days and they are very nice to me. I miss you all very much and wish I had wings so that I could fly over to you. I received a card from Willi and was very happy about it. It is obvious that he has not lost his sense of humor. I send your mother-in-law and rest of the family my best as well. That's it for today with a thousand kisses.

Your faithful and loving,

Mother

. . .

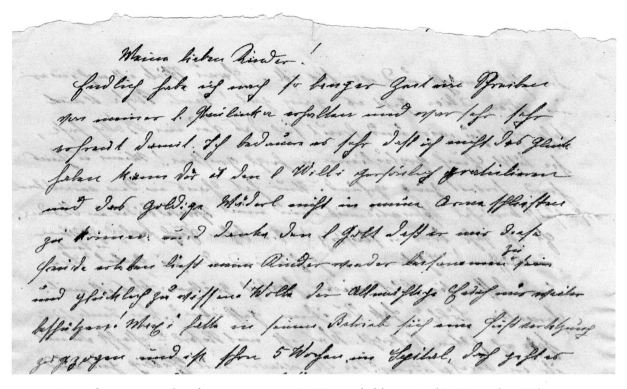

Letter from my grandmother to my parents in Nice probably received in November 1940.

My dear children,

Finally, after a long time, I received a letter from my beloved Paulinko, and I am answering right away. I regret so much not to be able to personally congratulate you and Willi, and not to be able to wrap my arms around that darling little girl. I thank the Almighty to have granted me the happiness to know that my children are together again and to know that they are happy. I think daily of you and can't wait for the time when I can hold you in my arms, which the dear Lord should grant us. I can imagine how happy you are with the child. We are well. I do not have any further news on our end. I often think of the baby, my first grandchild.

Max was injured at work and has been in the hospital for five weeks.* He is better, though, and I hope to have him home again in a few days. He is in a special workers' hospital and has excellent care; that makes me feel much better. I am well and have been accepted under Max's insurance coverage. That is worth a lot to me.

I kiss you a thousand times,

Your loving Mother

Kiss my darling little Jeannette a thousand times [God protect her!].

*Max was injured while doing hard labor on the railroads. Because letters were censored, people were afraid to write negative comments about their quality of life under the Nazi regime lest they get in trouble. For this reason, my grandmother and Max do not complain about the injury and the medical care.

Letter from my grandmother and Uncle Max, December 25, 1940.

My beloved good children,

I was, as always, so happy to hear from you, and often wish to be closer to you so that I could hold my sweet, dear little Jeannette in my arms. I miss all of you so much, but I have to console myself with the hope that I'll see you all again soon. Since yesterday, I have been with Mimi and Hans, and feel well here. We speak a lot about you and wish we could get more news. Mimi and Hans are very good to me and are very supportive. Max came home from the hospital but is still convalescing and not well yet. Tante Rosa visits me often, and sends regards. Rési is well. She gets together with Marianne, Gina, and another friend. She keeps knitting and sewing to avoid thinking about home. She is very homesick. I am happy that you got an affidavit to go to the USA [*that never materialized*]. Thousands of kisses,

Your Mom

Note from Max:

Dearest Paula and Willi,

First of all, I wish you, as well as little Jeannette and your loved ones, everything beautiful and good on the occasion of the holidays and New Year, most importantly good health. I am so happy that you have in your possession the affidavit that Paula Gutstein procured for you [*affidavit could not be used*]; at least this is a good beginning. It will be the most beautiful day when I will hear from you that you are happily settled in America and living a good life. I hope it won't take too long until the happy time when we will see each other again. You don't need to worry about Mama, Mimi, Hans, and I. We are doing fine and are healthy. Rési and Marianne are well; I receive mail from them every two to three weeks. They get together every other day. They always ask about you, as does Mrs. Robichek, and they all send their regards. Willi's sister, Paula, and her husband wrote from America to Rési last week. Everything is well with Phillip and Rési, and he writes her often. Tomorrow I will write to her and will forward your birthday wishes. I will inquire, as soon as possible, if I can send you a package of used clothing. Good holidays, cheers for the New Year, and best wishes. Write soon. Best regards. Kisses from your Max who always thinks of you. I kiss Mrs. Gerstl's hand [Mémé] and your family!

Max

Max and my grandmother on a visit to Tante Mimi and her husband, Hans, in Bad Voslau 1940.

Mimi wearing a cross. Her husband, who was Christian, convinced her to wear it to hide her religious identity. She remained in Austria undetected and survived. April 20, 1942

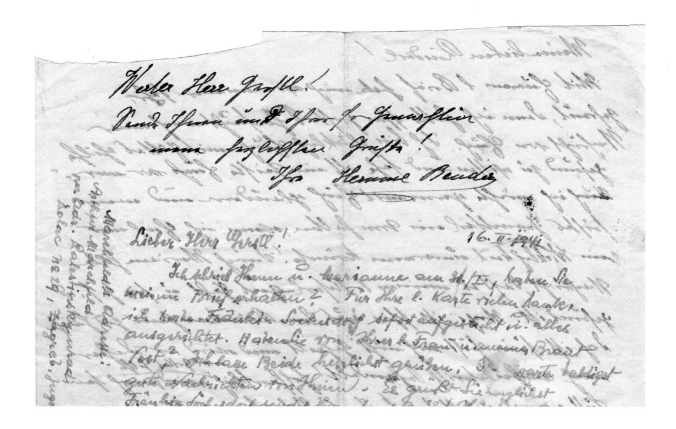

February 16, 1941

Dear Mr. Gerstl!

I wrote to you and Marianne on January 31st. Did you receive my letter? Many thanks for your nice card. Did you get any mail from your wife and my bride? I send both my best regards. Everyday I await good news from them. How is your brother Ernst?

Regards,

Max Bender

Dear Paula and dear Willi,

I thank you for your letter. I am happy that you and your little Jeannette are well. My foot is better but I am still considered incapacitated, and I still receive compensation that I use for Mama and my living expenses. It is possible that soon Mama and I will be able to travel to Uncle Lindenfeld's home. We are very hopeful that we can stay with Mimi and Hans a little longer.

Kisses,

Your Max

Letter from my grandmother probably written in March 1941.

My dear children,

As always, I was so happy to receive your letter as it confirms that my loved ones are healthy. I am pained that you have lost so much and now do not have the means to buy anything. If only I could help you! I think so often of you and cannot await the time when I will meet my darling little girl and see you. God should protect you and little Jeannette so that she will grow up big and strong. Otherwise nothing is new. Mimi and Hans and Max are very good to me and try not to upset me. Max was discharged from the hospital last week but cannot care for himself the way he was cared for in the hospital. He was probably discharged too soon and the wound on his ankle opened again, so he is back in the nursing home. I hope that this time he will heal well, and will be discharged on the first. Don't worry about me. I am receiving support money while he is in the hospital. It is of some help that protects us from need. Later, when he will be well, he will start to work again and things will return to normal. Rési is well and gets together with Marianne every week. She writes that she hasn't heard from you and asks if you have received her letters.

For today, live well and stay healthy.

With thousands of kisses,

Your faithful Mother.

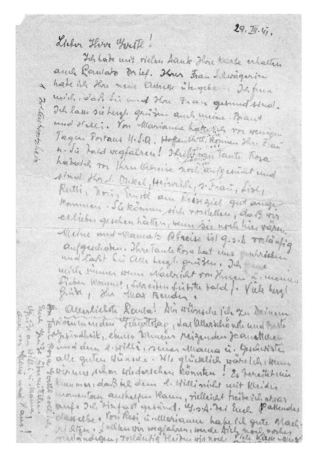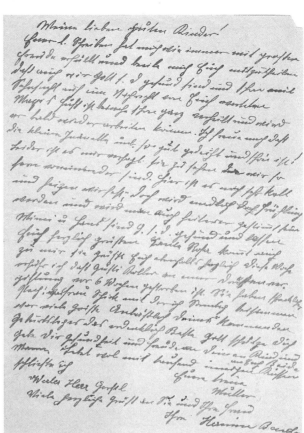

From my grandmother, March 29, 1941, and, on the reverse side, from Uncle Max.

My beloved good children,

Your letter filled me with joy, as usual, and I am hurrying to let you know that, thank God, we are also in good health, and were awaiting news from you with much longing. Max's foot is actually totally healed and he will soon be able to return to work. I am happy that little Jeannette is doing so well and is happy. Unfortunately, it is denied to me to see her, as we are so far away from each other. Mimi and Hans are well and send you their regards. As for your forthcoming birthday, I send you my best wishes for good health and happiness with your child and your husband. Live well, and thousands of kisses to both of you.

Your faithful Mother

Note from Max to Schié:

Dear Mr. Gerstl,

I received your card and Paula's letter and thank you very much. I visited your aunt Rosa, your Uncle Henry, and Lisl, Ruthi, Nori, and Ernst before they left. They all arrived safely to their new destination. You can imagine that we would have much preferred if they had been able to stay here. Our deportation, thank God, has been postponed at this time. I am always happy when I receive news from you and my loved ones. Please write soon. Best regards,

Yours,
Max Bender

Note to Ma:

Most beloved Paula,

For your forthcoming birthday I wish you the best of the best, and good health, as well as to the ravishing little Jeannette, and Willi, his mother and sisters and brothers. How happy I would be if we could see each other again. I feel so bad that I cannot help Willi with clothing at this time. Maybe I can send some of his patterns. I am almost well. I have good news from Rési and Marianne. Should we have to leave our home, I will let you know ahead of time; right now we are still staying here.

Many kisses,

Max

.   .   .

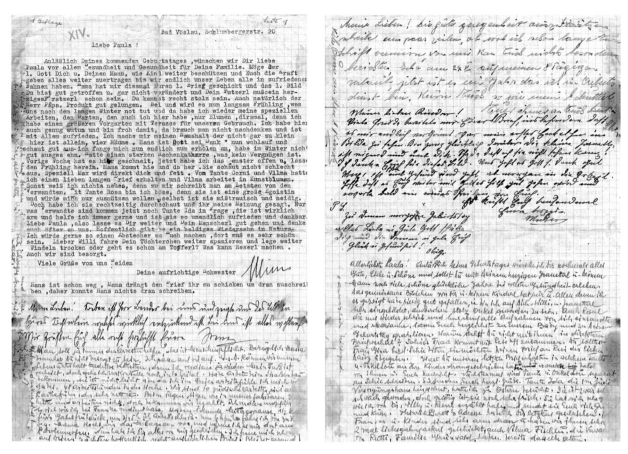

This letter was written from Bad Voslau, Schlumbergerstr. 20, Mimi's home, probably in early April 1941, before my mother's 32nd birthday and my parents' anniversary at the end of the month.

Note from my grandmother:

My dear children,

Much happiness awaited me when I received your letter, especially that I was granted to see my first little grandchild on a photograph. I am so happy about that. Little Jeannette is gorgeous and also fat. It's so sad that I cannot see her. I thank you for the letter. We are well, thank God. Max is also well by now and starts work tomorrow. I kiss you a thousand times,

Your faithful Mother

P.S. For your birthday tomorrow, best wishes. God protect you and yours and give you good luck and good health.

Note: From Max:

Most beloved Paula,

Regarding your birthday, my best wishes again, and you should have a long life filled with joy and happiness with your sweet little Jeannette and your husband. The picture of you and your child pleased me so much, as well as everyone I showed it to, and I am very proud of you, Willi, and little Jeannette, besides being proud of having become an uncle. Rési wrote recently and sent me pictures of herself and Marianne. She congratulates you on the birth of your baby and for your birthday. Uncle Henry, his wife and children are not doing well at all. They are very poor and we sent them two packages, as did Vilma Fischl and family Gruenwald. It is a human obligation to help the poor. Don't worry about Mother. I am taking care of her. Thank God we have enough for the necessities, as I am working again. My foot is healed but I still go for check-ups at the hospital. My work is at the streetcars. It is not easy but as I work outdoors, I feel good. I work 48 hrs. per week. There are ten Jewish workers and one non-Jewish controller who is very nice. When it rains, we sit in a hut and don't work, but I get paid anyway. I earn about as much as I earned at Franke. We get one hour for lunch and a half an hour morning break. I leave at six in the morning. Mama cooks my lunch and I warm it on a petroleum stove. So now I've written everything about myself. I am already happy awaiting your next detailed letter. Stay well. Max

Typewritten note from Mimi:

Dear Paula,

On the occasion of your birthday, I wish you, dear Paula, good health as well as for your family. God should continue to protect you, your husband and child, and give you the strength to continue until we can finally start to live our lives in happiness again. Mama sent me your letter this time and the picture. You look good and haven't changed at all, and your Putzele must be a cute little sweetie by now. You can be proud, naturally, also Sir Papa. Product well produced! Here, spring is slowly emerging which, after a long winter, is a relief. I have my special work cut out for me now, which is gardening. I grow flowers and lots of vegetables. I keep very busy and I am glad because it keeps me from thinking too much. I am finally starting to feel better. I had a bad cough and cold this winter which was no fun. It snowed last week and now my window is open to let the spring air in. Mama comes here once in awhile. She looks O.K., and Max is getting fat. Otherwise, I have no news as I am always the last one to get news from the family. So, dear Paula, continue to be well, also your little one, and think of us more often. Hopefully a reunion in the near future is destined for us. I would love to drop in on you — it must be beautiful over there. Dear Willi, keep taking your little daughter for walks and hang her diapers to dry — or does she go on the potty by now? Many kisses from both of us.

Your sister,

Mimi

· · ·

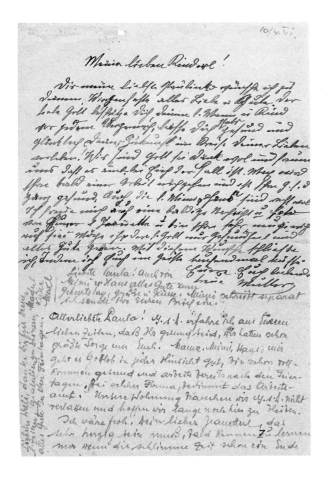

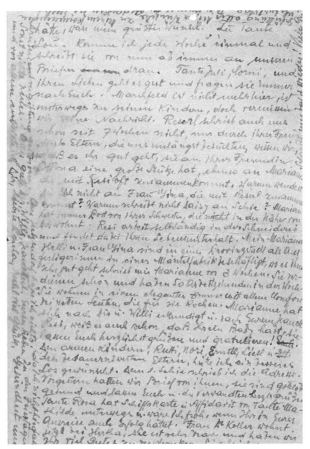

April 10, 1941

Most beloved Paula,

Thank goodness we received your letter letting us know that you are well. We were very worried. Mama, Mimi, Hans and I are in good health. I am totally well, and will start to work after the holidays. The employment agency will determine what company I will work for. We do not have to leave our apartment yet, and we hope that we can still remain here for a long time. I would be so happy to meet your darling little Jeannette soon; she is surely very cute. If only this terrible time would be over, that would be my biggest wish. Rési has not written for about seven weeks, but we know that she is well through her friend's parents who visited us recently. Her friend is a big help to her, as well as Marianne who sees her often. Why does she not give information to Gina who gets together with her often? Why does Rési not write to Schié directly? She works independently in tailoring now, and is earning decent wages. My Marianne and Gina work in a coat factory as finishers and they like it there. They get good wages and work fifty hours a week. They live in an elegant room with all comforts; the owners are nice people who cook for them. Marianne asks about you, Willi and Jeannette. Rési also knows that you had a baby. They send their best regards and congratulations. The poor children, Ruthi, Nori, Ernst, Lisl, and their parents — I would have wished them a better future. I wrote their address to Schié. I wish you well, you, Willi, Jeannette, and the rest of the family for the holidays, and mostly I wish you, dear Paula, the best for your birthday, luck, good health, and the realization of all your dreams. My thoughts are always with you. Write soon.

Much love,
Max

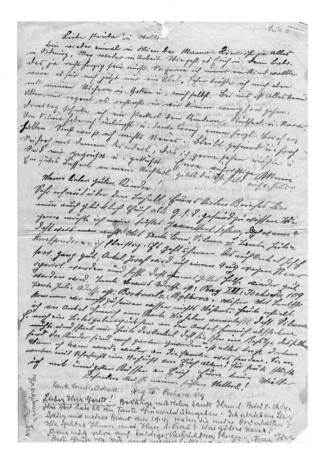
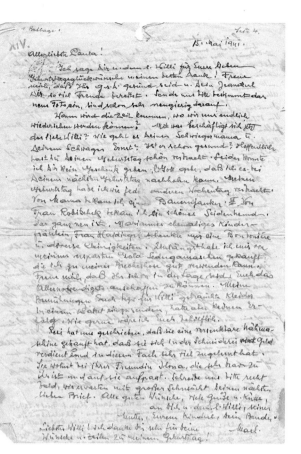

Note from Mimi, my grandmother, and Max

Dear Paula and Willi,

I am in Vienna with Mama again. Everything is O.K. Max is working again. How are you and the baby who must be so cute by now? As much as I always wanted children, now it would be too much trouble for me, so I console myself with my animals and my husband. Nothing is new here and it has been raining so much that we really can't go anywhere. I will be sending a package to Ruthi and Nora on Tuesday. I recently received a letter from Vilma and Tante Corni. Stay well and be happy with your child whom I am so anxious to see.

With many kisses,

Mimi

From my grandmother

My dear good children,

I was happy with your letter and the fact that you are well. How happy I would be to see my first grandchild, but when? That we do not know. I correspond with Tante Corni, Vilma and Tante Julia. Tante Corni's address is Prague XII, Fockgasse 109. Tante Julia's address is Boskowitz, Bylkowa. I received a card today from Uncle Henry. We heard that Vilma wants to send a package to him. If I can, I also will send something to the family. They are sure that they will hear from you. I close this letter with many kisses. Your mother.

Max to Schié:

Dear Mr. Gerstl,

Thank you for your letter of April 22nd. I forwarded your correspondence to Tante Grunwald. I wrote to her, to Rési, and to my fiancée on April 29th. Did you receive my mail? How are you and your wife? What is new? I am looking forward to receive mail from you soon. Best regards from my mother and me to you and your wife.

Max Bender

My most beloved Paula,

Many thanks for your good birthday wishes. I am happy that you are healthy and have so much joy with your little Jeannette. Please be sure to send me her new photograph. I can't wait to see it. When will the time come when we finally will be able to see each other again! What is Willi doing to keep busy these days? How is your mother-in-law and your brother-in-law Ernst? Is he healthy now? I hope you had a nice birthday. Unfortunately, I could not give you a gift. God should grant that I can make it up to you on your next birthday. I spent my birthday the same as any other weekday. Mama gave me a down jacket. I received a very nice silk shirt from Mrs. Robichek. Mrs. Hardinger, a friend of Marianne's, gave me a box of chocolates and other small gifts. I am happy that you now are in a position where you can provide yourselves with important necessities. I tried to find used clothing for Willi to send in a package, but had no luck. How happy I would be to be able to help you. Rési wrote that she bought a sewing machine and earns some money in dressmaking, and has learned very much in that trade. She lives with her friend, Ilona, who is very nice to her and watches over her. Write us soon. We await your letter and miss you very much.

Best wishes, regards and kisses to you, Willi, his mother, and your little child.

Your brother,

Max

• • •

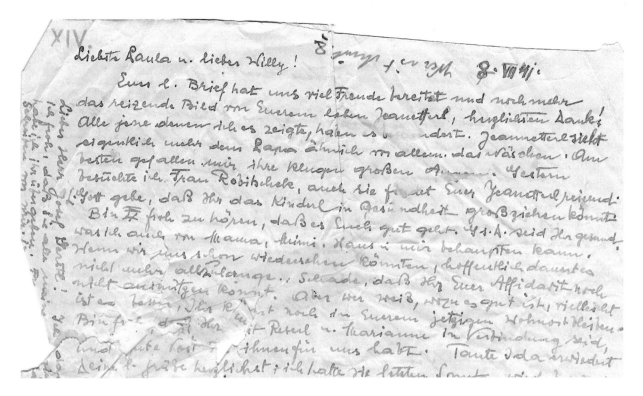

July 8, 1941

Dearest Paula and dear Willi,

Your letter brought us much joy and even more, the beautiful photograph of your little Jeannette. Many thanks. Everyone I show it to admires it. Actually, Jeannette looks more like her father, especially the little nose. She is adorable. God grant that you can raise her to adulthood in good health. I am happy to hear that you are well. Stay well, which I can state to be the case for Mama, Mimi, Hans and I. How I wish we could see each other again; hopefully it won't take too long for this to happen. Too bad that you cannot use your affidavit yet, but maybe it might be for the best.

I am happy that you communicate with Rési and Marianne. Vilma gave me a pair of nice, sturdy brown shoes last week, and I certainly can use them. Many regards from Mrs. Robichek. I sent a package to Uncle Henry for the family. I have not heard from them for eight weeks, and that worries me. I feel so sorry for the poor children. Give me the name of your landlady in Belgium so that I can write to her to inquire about your things. I received a letter two weeks ago from Rési and Marianne. Rési wishes you a belated happy birthday. She writes that she went through very hard times. I am somewhat satisfied with my work because at least I earn a little money, but it is very hard work. The place where I work is in a beautiful wooded region by the south train area, 16 km from home, so I have to get up at 3:45 A.M. My dear ones, how often I think how wonderful it would be if we could be together and I had the opportunity to see and admire your little girl in person. I would write to you more often and in more detail, but I am tired from my work and I cannot get enough sleep. Write me soon.

Many kisses, warm regards, and all the best to all of you.

Your Max

Letter from my grandmother and Uncle Max, probably August 1941. Top of letter is cut off.

From my grandmother:

My beloved good children,

I am answering your letter that made me so happy, as dear Willi related his experiences in such a humorous way. The child must be especially adorable now and I am often in your midst in my thoughts and imagine everything to be very lively there. This time, I don't have much news. Possibly we will soon have to leave our apartment. At this time, we don't have any details. I received news from Rési. She is, thank God, in good health. In the morning she does tailoring, and in the afternoons she is at her old job. I recently wrote to her that Phillip did not receive her letter. She met a very nice man who wants to marry her. I hope she is smart enough not to ruin that relationship.

I am well and think often of you. Max, Mimi and Hans are well.

Many kisses to all.

Your loyal and loving,
Mother

From Max:

Dear Paula and Willi,

Many thanks for your letters. We are always happy to receive mail from you. Your letters are very interesting, especially Willi's words which amused us very much. If only the war was over and we could all be together again and speak to each other in person. How wonderful that would be. I would be so happy to meet my little niece, Jeannette. She is so cute on the photograph. From your writing, she must be very cute and funny. Here everything is O.K. The most important is health. I always pray to the dear Lord that He protect all of us. From Rési and Marianne I get mail regularly. They send regards. Mrs. Greenwald and I sent clothing to the Henry Gerstl family. Willi's Tante Rosa and Uncle Henry asked us to send you regards, also from the children. Marianne lives near Rési. They work as cooks in a hotel. We are in contact with Tante Cornie and Vilma. Vilma sent me a pair of almost new shoes. She is also supporting the family of Henry Gerstl. She is a good person. Tante Rosa has an infection. I will write to your ex landlady to see if she can explain what happened to your belongings.

Otherwise not much new except that we soon will have to move to another apartment, but we don't know where yet. I work in road construction and feel well, as I work with nice people in a good neighborhood.

Mimi is a cook in a boarding house. Enough for today. Write soon.

Many regards and kisses, and best wishes,

Your Max

·   ·   ·

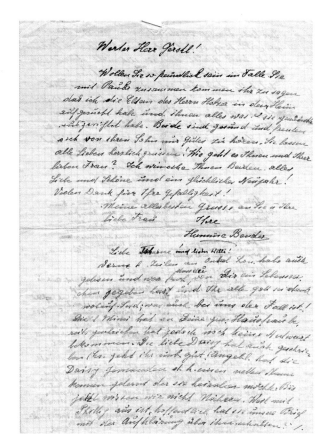

Written sometime in the fall of 1941

From my grandmother to Schié:

Dear Mr. Gerstl,

Would you please be so kind to tell Paula that I visited Mr. Holzer's parents, and gave them all the information that they wanted. They are both healthy and were happy to hear that their son is well. Please give my regards to everyone. How are you and your wife? I wish you the best and a happy New Year. Many thanks for your favor. Best regards to you and your dear wife.

Hermine Bender

Dear Tscharne [Ma's Jewish name], dear Willi,

I read your kind words to Uncle Lou and I was happy to see a sign of life on your part. I am glad that all of you are well, thank God, as am I. Mimi wrote to your ex landlady in Belgium, but has not received an answer yet. Rési wrote to me and she is well. It seems that she met a nice man who would like to marry her. At this time, we don't know anything more. Phillip and her are no longer together. I hope she received our letter. Rési deserves a different man than Phillip. He is having a relationship with another young woman and thinks that Rési doesn't care. Who knows why things happen. I hope to hear from you soon and am already happy in anticipation. Live well and I kiss you, your dear husband and your child.

From your Mother

Dear Mr. Joseph [Schié's given name],

I also wish you, your dear wife, your mother, siblings, dear Marianne, and Rési the best for the New Year. Did you receive my card and letter dated September 12? My mother wrote to my sister, Paula, on August 11. Unfortunately that letter was not delivered and was returned to us.

Best regards,

Max Bender

P.S.: Please send this letter to Tscharne. It will save us from writing again.

Again from Max:

Dear Tscharne, dear Willi, dear little Jeannette,

Uncle Lou informed us that you are concerned about us. We were worried about you as well. Please write soon. I wish you good health and the best for the New Year, and my wish is that we will soon all be together again. I got mail from Rési and Marianne and they are well. We visited Tante Corni yesterday who is very nice and hospitable. She helps us very much. I am still working on the streetcars at the South train station 22 kms from home. The Gerstl family, Ruthi, Nori, Lisl are well. Ruthi asks for a letter from you. She still loves you very much. How are you and little Jeannette?

Kisses from your Max

• • •

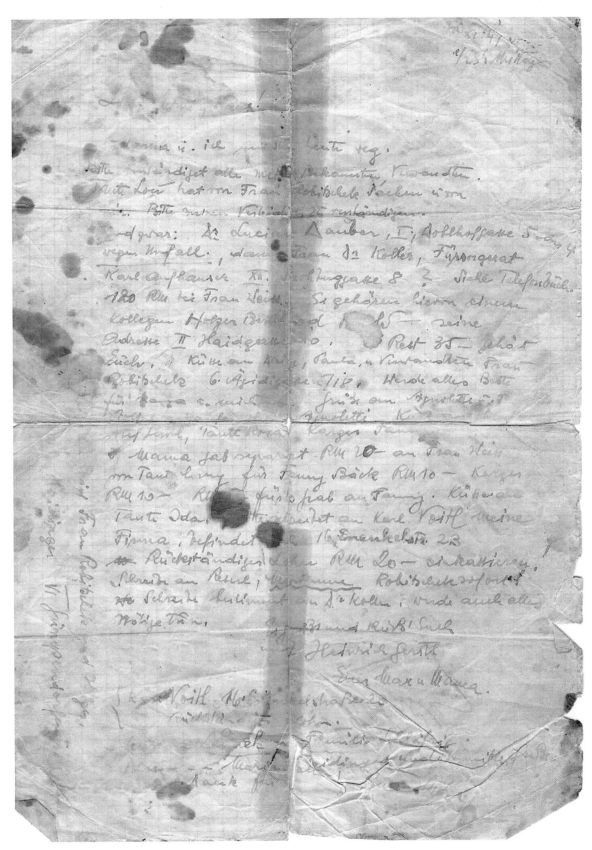

This is the last correspondence from Uncle Max. It is a letter of good-bye to his sister Mimi and all the people he loved. My grandmother and Max were about to be picked up from their home by the Gestapo. In 1957, my mother found out that they were deported to Riga, Latvia. After this letter, my grandmother and uncle were never heard from again.

[*Translation from previous page*]

November 30, 1941, 1 o'clock in the afternoon

Dear Hans and Mimi!

Mother and I must leave today. Please notify all my friends and relatives. Tante Lou has some things from Mrs. Robichek and some of my things. Please let the following people know: Dr. Lucien Aubar, [address] regarding the accident, also Mrs. Dr. Koler [address], attorney Carl Aufhauser. Look up his address in the telephone book. Mrs. Weiss has 120 RM [Reichmarks] that belong to a colleague; 85 RM belong to Holzer Bernhard. The rest, 35 marks, belongs to you. Kisses to Rési, Paula and family, and Mrs. Robichek. I will do the best for Mama and me. Regards to Joseph Gerstl, Tante Rosa, the Kargas family. Mama gave 20 RM separately to Mrs. Weiss from Tante Cornie, for Fanny Baek 10 RM, 10 RM to Fanny for the grave. Kisses to Tante Ida. Please write to my boss Karl Voitl [address] and collect 20 RM, write to Rési and Marianne Robichek immediately. Absolutely write to Dr. Koller who will also do everything necessary for you.

Regards and kisses,

Your Max and Mama

• • •

AMT DER WIENER LANDESREGIERUNG
Magistrats-Abteilung 12
mittelbare Bundesverwaltung
(Referat Opferfürsorge)

M.Abt. 12-G 285/57   Wien, am 25.Nov.1957
GERSTL Wilhelm,
Opferfürsorge

              An
                    Herrn Wilhelm G e r s t l ,

                              3323 Sturtevant
                              Detroit 6 Michigan
                              U.S.A.

         In Beantwortung Ihres Schreibens vom 8.10.1957 wird mitgeteilt,
dass die Israelitische Kultusgemeinde Wien Ihre Vertretung übernommen
hat und Sie von dort die nähere Auskunft betreffend Ihres Opfer-
fürsorge-Ansuchens erhalten werden.
         Bezüglich des Verbleibens Ihrer Angehörigen wird unten berichtet.
Ueber Rosa Geiringer konnte keine Auskunft eingeholt werden, da
4 Personen gleichen Namens in der Deportationskartei aufscheinen
und daher Personaldaten bei Auskunftserteilung bekannt sein müssen.
Hermine BENDER, geb.Baeck,) wurden am 3.12.1941 nach Riga
Max BENDER   ) deportiert und liegt über ihre
                                   Rückkehr keine Nachricht auf.
                    Für den Landeshauptmann:

A.D.Nr. 1105B - 10 - 576 - 28925 - D.B.

HERMINE BENDER AND MAX BENDER

… DEPORTED TO RIGA AND NEVER RETURNED …

THE BUREAU OF VIENNESE PROVINCIAL GOVERNMENT
Magistrate-Department 12
Federal Adminisration
Department of Research of Victims

Vienna, November 25, 1957

To Mr. Wilhelm Gerstl

        Regarding your letter of October 8, 1957, we are informing you that the
Israeli Community Bureau in Vienna has taken over your inquiry, and you will
receive a more precise answer from them. Please see below for information
regarding your family. We could not find any information regarding Rosa
Geiringer because four people in the deportation file had the same name. The
Reference Department therefore needs more personal data.
        Hermine BENDER, née Baeck)   were deported to Riga on December 3,
        Max BENDER   ) 1941, and there is no record of return.

              For the Head Bureau Manager,

                    Signature ......

Historical Information

Riga, Latvia: Hitler's Final Solution Takes
Hermine Bender and Max Bender

In my search to find out what happened to my Uncle Max and grandmother Hermine, I sent the following e-mail to the site "Jewish Traces," and their reply follows my message.:

----- Original Message -----
From: jolsons
To: jewishtraces@jewishtraces.org
Sent: Monday, April 30, 2012 9:43 PM
Subject: Hermine Bender and Max Bender

Taken from Vienna on December 3rd, 1941. Taken to a ghetto in Vienna, and from there Jungfernhof in Latvia. No return. Do you know any more? Any information would be most appreciated. They are my grandmother and uncle. Jeannette Olson

From: jewish traces
To: jolsons
Date: Friday, June 01, 2012 10:58 PM
Subject: Friday, June 01, 2012 11:58 PM

Dear Jeannette,

Thank you for your email. In order to get the type of answer you are looking for you should write to ITS in Bad Arolsen and/or to the USHMM archives in DC (if you live in the US) providing the birth date of both of them and place of birth. The DOW in Vienna might also give you more information. A page of testimony was left in Yad Vashem by Pauline Gerstl (your mother?)

Max Bender was born in Wien, Austria in 1907 to Sigmund and Hermine nee Bek. He was a bookkeeper and single. Prior to WWII he lived in Wien, Austria. During the war he was in Wien, Austria. Max was murdered in the Shoah.

Manuela Wyler

In Riga, the capital of Latvia that was annexed by the Soviet Union in 1940, there lived 43,600 Jews in 1935, which corresponded to 11.3 percent of the population. Excesses directed against the Jewish population followed immediately after the invasion by German troops on 1 July 1941. After the introduction of numerous discriminatory decrees, and after plunderings and massacres, the ghetto was installed and surrounded by a wall in September/October 1941.

Between the end of November and the beginning of December 1941, 27,000 Jews, most of them from Latvia, but including about 400 elderly people from Vienna, were shot in Rumbula forest. In this way space was to be provided for fresh transports from Germany and Austria.

Transports with total of 4200 Jews arrived from Austria in Riga after a journey lasting 8 days, on 3 December 1941 and on 11 and 26 January and 6 February 1942. The deportees were put into those areas of the ghetto which had been emptied by the murder program or else had to perform forced labor in the outpost of Salaspils. The mortality rate of those interned in the ghetto rose sharply because of the frightful living conditions, particularly among the weaker ones, but above all among the elderly and the children.

When on 6 February 1942 the last transport from Vienna arrived in Riga, on arrival at Skrotave station those to whom the kilometre-long march on foot to the ghetto seemed too exhausting were offered lorries — which in fact were camouflaged gas vans — to travel to the ghetto. Of 1000 deportees from Vienna, only 300 reached the ghetto on foot.Only about 800 of the 20,000 men, women and children deported to Riga survived the selection for forced labour, the ghetto and the various concentration camps, and among them were about 100 Austrian Jews.

• • •

The following two records of death were included in Manuela Wyler's e-mail, as well as the information that follows. She forwarded this from Yad Vashem's [Israel's Holocaust Museum] website.

Namentliche Erfassung der oesterreichischen Holocaustopfer, Dokumentationsarchiv des oesterreichischen Widerstandes (Documentation Centre for Austrian Resistance), Wien	
Last Name:	Bender
First Name:	Hermine
Gender (according to given name):	Female
Date of Birth:	08/02/1872
Place of Birth:	Grossmeseritsch, Velke Mezirici, Moravia-Silesia, Czechoslovaki
Place during the war:	Wien, Vienna, Austria
Wartime Address:	WIEN 2, SCHOENERERSTRASSE 42/5
Details of transport:	Transport 13 from Wien, Vienna, Austria to Riga, Rigas, Vidzeme
קישור לשילוח:	Transport 13 from Wien, Vienna, Austria to Riga, Rigas, Vidzeme
Prisoner Nr. in Transport:	212
Type of material:	List of murdered Jews from Austria
Victims' status end WWII:	murdered/perished
Item ID:	4928462

Documentation of death, Max Bender and Hermine Bender

(Documentation Centre for Austrian Resistance), Wien	
Last Name:	Bender
First Name:	Max
Gender (according to given name):	Male
Date of Birth:	21/04/1907
Place of Birth:	Wien, Vienna, Austria
Place during the war:	Wien, Vienna, Austria
Wartime Address:	WIEN 2, SCHOENERERSTRASSE 42/5
Details of transport:	Transport 13 from Wien, Vienna, Austria to Riga, Rigas, Vidzeme, Latvia on 03/12/1941
Prisoner Nr. in Transport:	213
Type of material:	List of murdered Jews from Austria
Victims' status end WWII:	murdered/perished
Item ID:	4928465

Source: *Internet. Wikepedia, Riga Ghetto.*

At the end of 1941 and the beginning of 1942, Latvia received 15,000 Jewish deportees from Germany, Austria, Czechoslovakia, and other annexed countries; they were the "Reich" [German Empire] Jews. The Reich Jews were not immediately housed in the ghetto, but rather they were left at a provisional concentration camp established at Jumpravmuiza, also known as Jungfrauhof. Of the approximately 4,000 people transported to Jungfrauhof, only 148 persons survived. December 1st to December 8, 1941, four trainloads of Jews deported from the Reich arrive in Riga and are housed initially at Jungfrauhof under atrocious conditions; many are shot by the Aryan commandos in the Biķernieki forest.

Jungfrauhof concentration camp	
Also known as	Mazjumprava, KZ Jungfrauhof
Location	near Riga, Latvia
Date	December 1941 to March 1942
Incident type	Imprisonment without trial, mass shootings, forced labor, starvation, exile
Perpetrators	*Franz Walter Stahlecker; Rudolph Seck
Organizations	Nazi SS, Latvian Auxiliary Police
Victims	About 4,000 German and Austrian Jews
Survivors	About 148 people
Memorials	At Bikernieki Forest

The Jungfrauhof concentration camp was an improvised concentration camp in Latvia, at the Mazjumprava Manor, near the Šķirotava Railway Station about three or four kilometers from Riga (now within the city territory). The camp was in operation from December 1941 through March 1942, and served as overflow housing for Jews from Germany and Austria, who had originally had been intended for Minsk as a destination.

The former estate of 200 hectares in size, had built on it a warehouse, three large barns, five small barracks and various cattle sheds. The partially falling down and unheatable buildings were unsuitable for the accommodation of several thousand people. There were no watchtowers or enclosing perimeter, rather a mobile patrol of ten to fifteen Latvian auxiliary police under the German commandant Rudolf Seck.

In December 1941 a total of 3,984 people were brought in four separate trains to Jungfrauhof, including 136 children under ten years old, and 766 elders. On December 1, 1941, 1,013 Jews from Württemberg were entrained and sent to the camp. Further transports came from Nuremberg with 1,008 persons and Vienna with 1,001.

Einstzgruppe A (Death Squad A) Franz Walter Stahlecker, Commandant

After the annexation of Austria in 1938, Franz Walter Stahlecker became Security Service chief of the Danube district (Vienna). In June 1941 Stahlecker was promoted to SS-Brigade leader and General major of the Police. He was the commanding officer of Einsatzgruppe A, the most murderous of four death squads active in German-occupied Eastern Europe. Einsatzgruppe A's mission was to hunt down and annihilate the Jews, Gypsies, Communists, and other "undesirables." The official full name is Einsatzgruppen der Sicherheitspolizei und des SD (Task Force of the Security Police and Main Security Office.) These were SS paramilitary death squads that were responsible for mass killings, typically by shooting of Jews in particular, but also significant numbers of other population groups and political categories. The Einsatzgruppen operated throughout the territory occupied by the German armed forces following the German invasions of Poland, in September, 1939, and later, of the Soviet Union on June 22, 1941. The Einsatzgruppen carried out operations ranging from the murder of a few people to operations which lasted over two or more days, such as the massacres at Babi Yar (33,771 killed in two days) and Rumbula, Latvia, (25,000 killed in two days). The Einsatzgruppen were responsible for the murders of over 1,000,000 people, and they were the first Nazi organizations to commence mass killing of Jews as an organized policy.

By winter 1941, Stahlecker reported to Berlin that Einsatzgruppe A had murdered some 249,420 Jews. He was killed in action on 23 March 1942, in a clash with Soviet partisans in Russia.

• • •

"Jewish Executions Carried Out by Einsatzgruppe A"

Coffins illustrate the number of murdered Jews

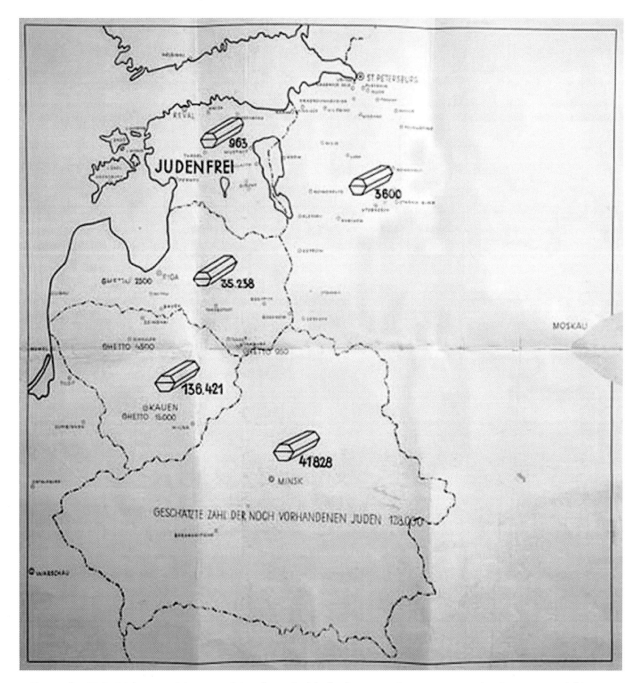

From the U.S. Holocaust Museum: Map from Stahlecker's report, January 31, 1942. It is stamped "Secret Reich Matter." It summarizes 220,250 murders committed by Einsatzgruppe A under his command in the Baltic States and Belarus in 1941. The legend at the bottom states that "the estimated number of Jews still on hand is 128,000." Estonia is marked as "judenfrei" [free of Jews].

Document held in the Latvian State Historical Archives, Riga.

EPILOGUE

My father died in 1993, five years after I concluded the interviews. He was eighty-nine. My mother died in 2006, at ninety-six. A couple of years before her death, she no longer clearly remembered the war years. Periodically, she would ask me how her mother and brother died. Not wanting to upset her, I would answer that they passed away of old age. Sometimes she would remember and respond, "No, they were killed."

Cécile and I reunited in Vienna, 1949.

After leaving Vence in 1947, we settled in Cannes for a few years. Because of the uncertainty of getting visas, my parents frequently talked about the option of returning to Austria. I witnessed many arguments during these discussions. Mémé, Cécile, Tante Rosa, Uncle Ludwig, and Uncle Ernie had returned there in 1948. My father wanted to join his family in his homeland, but my mother, with good reason, now hated Austria and the Austrians. She could neither forgive nor forget what they had done to her, to her family, and to the Jews. She wanted a new beginning elsewhere, a place where she would not be living with ghosts of the past for the rest of her life. To please my father, in 1949, she agreed to a trip to Vienna to investigate the possibility of moving there. Uncle Ludwig owned a men's clothing store, and had a job waiting for my father. I loved Cécile and was excited about the possibility of living close to her.

While in Vienna, my parents looked at an apartment that Uncle Ludwig had found for them. It was small and dark, and in a noisy neighborhood — a far cry from the apartment where we lived in Cannes, a light and airy third-floor dwelling in a charming house belonging to an older couple, Paul and Delphine Rondel. From our balcony, we could see palm trees, small picturesque homes with lovely gardens, and beyond, the beautiful waters of the Mediterranean. The people who were vacating the apartment in Vienna were leaving for the United States. This was the proverbial "nail in the coffin" for my mother. We would be moving into this depressing place, surrounded by people she would never trust, while the vacating family was going where she desperately wanted to go. She stood firm about her decision, and we returned to Cannes. In August 1951, thirteen years after my parents had initiated their efforts to reach the shores of America, we were finally granted our visas — I was almost eleven. On November 13th, we loaded our two suitcases into a taxi that took us to the pier in Cannes. We boarded the steamship, Vulcania, and bid farewell to Europe.

After a tumultuous thirteen-day voyage across the Atlantic, we arrived in New York on November 27, 1951. We stayed with my mother's uncle, Max Lindenfeld, for two weeks. He was in his eighties and lived alone in an apartment in Manhattan that was similar to the one my mother had turned down in Vienna. I thoroughly disliked that apartment, as I did New York, which I found bewildering and overwhelming compared to quiet, little Cannes. My mother wanted to remain in New York, but my father didn't. She loved city life, as she had loved life in Vienna many years before. My father, however, wanted to be with his sister, Paula, her husband, and their daughter, Ruthie, who lived in Detroit. This time, my father got his way, much to my mother's chagrin. We got on a train, left New York, and arrived in Detroit on December 11, 1951, a cold and snowy

Michigan day. We stepped off the train and came face to face with new opportunities that would provide us with a good life in the United States.

- Henry and Hilda lived out their days in Nice. They remained childless.

- Schié and Gina [his wife] came to the United States a few years after us. They settled in New Jersey and remained childless.

- Ernst moved to New Jersey in 1959 where he lived out his life near Schié and Gina. He never remarried.

- Rosa, Ludwig, and Cécile moved back to Vienna from Nice in 1948. They raised Cécile but had no other children.

- Cécile remained in Vienna and married Robert Gruenwald. They had two children, Natalie and Alexander. They were blessed with seven grandchildren.

- Mémé moved to Vienna with Rosa and Ludwig, and continued to live with them until her death in 1973, age ninety-nine.

- Ruthe Gutstein married Richard Bardos and had three children, Lori, David and Sally. They had seven grandchildren.

- From the seven children born to Mémé, there were only three offsprings: Ruthe, Cécile, and me. We each had seven grandchildren.

- My mother lost her mother, her brother, cousins, aunts and uncles at the hands of the Nazis. Her sister Theresa, who had fled to England, married there and moved to Argentina in the 1950s. She had two children, Ralph, born in England, and Jennie, born in Argentina. They immigrated to Detroit in the late 1960s.

- My mother's sister Mimi never left Vienna. She remained childless.

At the time of this writing in 2012, Andrée, granddaughter of Delphin and Antoinette Picco, and daughter of Marguerite and Eugene Francone, lives in Lyon, France, with her husband Pierre-Bernard Blumet. She has two sons and two daughters, and quite a few grandchildren. She wrote me in the year 2000 asking if we had any written documentation regarding her grandparents' and parents' role in saving my mother and father. She wanted to leave that as a legacy to her children. This initiated my efforts to provide her with official documentation. I submitted an application to the Holocaust Museum, Yad Vashem, in Israel, and it took them one year to validate our story. In November 2002, Andrée received notice that her mother, Mme Francone, in her nineties at the time and living in a nursing home in Vence, was to be presented with Medals of Honor and Honorary Diplomas issued by the state of Israel, the highest honor presented to those who had saved Jewish lives. She, and posthumously, her husband, Eugene, and her parents, Delphin and Antoinette Picco, were to be commemorated as "Righteous Among the Nations.*" A ceremony with high-profile guests such as the Israeli Ambassador to France, the mayor of Vence, and other

French and Israeli dignitaries, as well as family members and friends, was planned. Sadly, Mme Francone passed away five days prior to the event, and unfortunately it had to take place without her. The awards were presented to Andrée Blumet and her brother, Jean-Pierre Francone.

Lily moved to Paris before we left for the United States. She took a position as concierge of an apartment building on the Avenue du Président Wilson. She lived a lonely and difficult life, according to her letters. We never had the opportunity to see each other again, but we kept in touch regularly by mail. Shortly before Lily died in the late 1960s, she sent me photographs and the gold chain I wore while I lived with her. She replaced the Virgin Mary pendant on the chain with another ornament.

I am extremely grateful to my mother for keeping the volumes of correspondence and documentation relating to our family before and during WWII. By showcasing these historical documents and recording "The Story," I hope to have memorialized her account of what our family endured during the heinous, murderous regime of Adolph Hitler, and the heroic efforts of those who saved us.

Vienna, Austria, year 2000
Cécile, Ruthe and me
Cousins by birth, sisters at heart.

"Righteous Among the Nations" diplomas and medals of honor awarded to the Picco/Francone family from Yad Vashem in Israel.

*One of Yad Vashem's principal duties is to convey the gratitude of the State of Israel and the Jewish people to non-Jews who risked their lives to save Jews during the Holocaust. This mission was defined by the law establishing Yad Vashem, and in 1963 the Remembrance Authority embarked upon a worldwide project to grant the title of Righteous Among the Nations to the few who helped Jews in the darkest time in their history. To this end, Yad Vashem set up a public commission, headed by a Supreme Court Justice, which examines each case and is responsible for granting the title. Those recognized receive a medal and a certificate of honor and their names are commemorated.

STATISTICS

How Many Jews Were Deported From France to the Death Camps During WWII?

Source: Internet. *Answers.com.*

All numbers are approximate, but the estimate is that about 75,000 Jews were deported from France to death camps. Other estimates are somewhat higher, e.g. 77,000. Some of those deported from France were already refugees from other countries.

About 250,000 Jews in France survived the war. Yad Vashem has honored about 2,000 French people for protecting Jews from both the Nazis and the far right wing Vichy government. The Vichy regime represented the most virulent strains of anti-Semitism in France.

The Vichy eagerness to cooperate with the Nazis is sometimes seen as evidence of general French collaboration in gathering deportees. Jewish refugees who fled to Vichy-governed France usually found themselves worse off than in German-occupied areas.

While many were anti-Semitic at different levels, there was resistance in many areas to surrendering French citizens to the Germans, leading people to hide Jews.

The deportations shocked some into action. Despite the apathy or anti-Semitism of some church leaders, some French bishops bravely preached against the deportations at a critical time leading to more assistance for those in hiding.

Many French Jews were assimilated and not easily identified. The Germans had one million troops in occupied France, a ratio of about 1-40. That was an overwhelming force in military terms, but without greater French cooperation, the move to identify Jews and ship them to death camps was considerably hampered. While it is small consolation, the number of deaths could have been far higher.

Source: Internet. *ARC "Aktion Reinhard Camps", The French Deportation Camps Drancy and Gurs.*

"More than 3000 Jews died in France during the occupation, 2500 of them in the various camps in the Occupied Zone and the Free Zone. Of the 76,000 Jews deported from France, fewer than 3,000 survived."

THE FRANCONE/BLUMET FAMILY

Jean-Pierre Francone, Andrée's brother, at Andrée and her husband
Pierre-Bernard's 50th wedding anniversary party. August 2013.

Andrée and Pierre-Bernard Blumet [very back of photo], and their children and grandchildren, descendants of
Delphin and Antoinette Picco and Eugene and Marguerite Francone. Lyon, France, 2011

THE GERSTL/OLSON FAMILY

Jerry and Jeannette Olson and family, West Bloomfield, Michigan, 2012.

Left to right, front row: Aidan Sachs, Sheldon Olson, Max Olson

Middle row: Jonah Sachs, Jerry Olson, Justin William Sachs, Jeannette Olson, Joseph Olson

Back row: Louis Paul Light, Susan Bitnias, Jeffrey Bitnias, Stacey Sachs, Adam Sachs, Hilary Mechler holding her daughter Jordin Cherna Lily Mechler, Charles Mechler, Lauren Mechler

There are no remains.
Just a stone.

This headstone was erected by my mother in June 1997 in memory of her mother and brother. She chose the site adjacent to the one that was reserved for her. My father died in 1993 and my mother in 2006.

Adat Shalom Cemetery, Farmington Hills, Michigan.

About the Author

Jeannette Gerstl Olson was a hidden child during WWII. Born in Nice, France, in 1940, she survived the war hidden by Lily and Emile Lasfargues, a childless Christian French couple who wished to save her life and was ready to adopt her, had her parents lost their lives at the hands of the Nazis. She was reunited with her mother and father after the liberation in 1944, and they immigrated to the United States in 1951.

Taking advantage of her linguistic skills, Jeannette graduated from Wayne State University in Detroit, majoring in French and English, and earning a degree in Secondary Education. She married Jerry Olson in 1961. Her teaching career was limited due to her growing family, one son and three daughters. She now has seven grandchildren ranging in age from four to nineteen.

Presently, Jeannette is enjoying semi-retirement from her long-term position in a medical practice where she writes and designs in-house publications. She continues to speak at the Holocaust Memorial Center Zekelman Campus in Farmington Hills, Michigan, sharing her story with thousands of school children and adults for the past twelve years. She and Jerry love to travel, and together they have achieved their mission to retrace her parents' footsteps in Austria and France during the war years via numerous pilgrimages to Europe.

Recording "The Story"— as she refers to her parents' experiences during the Holocaust — and finally placing the plethora of her mother's documentation that is now approximately seventy-five years old into book form, have allowed Jeannette to pass on this personal piece of history to her children and grandchildren, and hopefully to future generations. Her mother, Pauline Gerstl, felt compelled to save documents, letters, photos, and other miscellaneous paper artifacts relating to her personal experiences during the war years, and it wasn't in vain. This precious collection is now the voice that accompanies the tale of *Maybe One Day*.

· · ·